GLORY
IN THE
CHURCH

GLORY
IN THE
CHURCH

Edited by Thomas and Sheila Jones

ILLUMINATION PUBLISHERS

Glory in the Church: Powerful Daily Readings Exploring the Eternal Plan for the Family of God.
© 2023 by Illumination Publishers International. Previously published by Discipleship Publications International in 1996.

Cover design: Toney C. Mulhollan.
Interior Layout: Anita Costello.

ISBN: 978-1-958723-05-0.

Edited by Tom A. and Sheila Jones. Sheila passed from this life in 2022. Tom Jones now makes his home in the city of Tuscaloosa, Alabama where he has helped start a new church planting. Some of Tom A Jones' other books include *No One Like Him, Deep Convictions, One Another, The Baptized Life, Glory in the Church, Mind Change, Mind Change Moments, The Kingdom of God, Volumes 1-3, The Prideful Soul's Guide to Humility* and many others.

To Al and Gloria Baird

CONTENTS

Introduction: God Has Cried Enough...................... 9

Part I *Born in Eternity*

1 Foreseen by Prophets
   G. Steve Kinnard 14
2 Built by Jesus
   Thomas Jones 18
3 Bought at a Price
   Gordon Ferguson 22
4 Led by the Savior
   Russ Ewell 26
5 Loved As a Wife
   Kay McKean 30
6 Sent into the World
   John Louis 34

Part II *Designed for Impact*

7 Where Truth Really Matters
   Rick Maule 40
8 Where Silence Is Not an Option
   Doug Webber 44
9 Where Love Is Supreme
   Jeff Chacon 48
10 Where Fellowship Is Rich
   Steve Staten 52
11 Where Race Never Matters
   Javier Amaya 56
12 Where Family Is Restored
   Jimmy Rogers 60
13 Where Gifts Differ
   Douglas Jacoby 64
14 Where Unity Is a Passion
   Nick Young 68

15 Where the Strong Love the Weak
   Mark Ottenweller, M.D. 72
16 Where Leaders Are Servants
   Mark Templer 76
17 Where Followers Bring Joy
   Brian Felushko 80

Part III *Directed to Love*

18 Loving One Another Deeply
   Kevin McDaniel 86
19 Accepting One Another
   Brian Scanlon 90
20 Devoted to One Another
   Debbie McDaniel 94
21 Greeting One Another
   Sheila Jones 98
22 Carrying Each Other's Burdens
   Dave Malutinok 102
23 Speaking the Truth in Love
   Jeanie Shaw 106
24 Submitting to One Another
   Kelly Petre 110
25 Admonishing and Teaching One Another
   Mike Fontenot 114
26 Encouraging One Another Daily
   Theresa Ferguson 118
27 Spurring One Another On
   Terrie Fontenot 122
28 Confessing Sins to Each Other
   Dean Farmer 126
29 Forgiving Each Other
   Adrienne Scanlon 130
30 Offering Hospitality to One Another
   Ron Brumley 134
31 Honoring One Another
   Richard Bellmor 138

Epilogue: Glory in the Church 142

God Has Cried Enough

In the minds of most people the word "church" does not conjure up images of something grand, something glorious, something powerful or something amazing. The wife of Robert A. Taft, the American politician, once remarked: "I always find that statistics are hard to swallow and impossible to digest. The only one I can ever remember is that if all the people who go to sleep in church were laid end to end, they would be a lot more comfortable." She summed up what a lot of people feel: Church is a place to sleep.

Ralph G. Ingersoll, the 19th-century attorney, gave a different but equally negative and equally common view when he wrote, "The Church has always been willing to swap off treasures in heaven for cash down below." Ralph Waldo Emerson found the church most attractive when it was sitting quietly and doing nothing. "I like the silent church before the service begins, better than any preaching," he wrote in an 1841 essay. But leave it to H.L. Mencken, the 20th-century American journalist, to bring the strongest charge: "A church is a place in which gentlemen who have never been to heaven brag about it to persons who will never get there." He thought the church to be a place either full of hypocrites or fools or, most likely, both.

So mention the church to many people, and a host of unattractive words jump into their minds—words like boredom, irrelevancy, greed, hypocrisy and foolishness. From the towering (but now empty) cathedrals of Europe to the picturesque white church buildings of New England (and Christmas card fame), the church has often been admired more for architecture than for attitude, more for construction than for character. It must make God cry.

Paul understood what the church could be—what God designed her to be—and that understanding comes through clearly in these words from his letter to the Ephesians:

> Now to him who is able to do immeasurably more than all we ask or imagine, according to his power that is at work within us,

to him be glory in the church and in Christ Jesus throughout all
generations, for ever and ever! Amen (Ephesians 3:20-21).

The true church is the instrument of the immeasurable one,
the chosen vessel of him who has all the power; and when the
church is true to her calling, the very power of God will work
in her, and there will be *glory in the church.* "I love the house
where you live, O LORD," David wrote in Psalm 26:8, "the place
where your glory dwells." But where does God's glory dwell in
our day? In the church, says Paul. No, not in empty edifices or
cozy sanctuaries, but in the people of God who have been
brought together by the blood of Jesus Christ, who have
committed themselves to a life of daily cross-bearing, and who
now look at life, at each other and at their neighbors in a totally
different way.

And so to this very day, almost 2,000 years since Jesus came
on the scene, the true church of Jesus Christ is an impressive
sight. It may be fourteen people crowded into an apartment in
a former Communist republic; it may be 13,000 souls overflow-
ing a famous arena in America, or it may be an interracial crowd
singing and celebrating in the city hall of Johannesburg, South
Africa, but if the heart of Jesus Christ is in the people, there will
be glory in the church. The glory will be so real and so bright
that it will not escape the newcomer. He may wonder at first if
this much love can be real. She may wonder if some kind of
mind control has led to such remarkable unity. He may ask
what has come over these teenagers who seem to be so close to
their parents. She may suspect that something sinister lurks
behind the scenes, for "nothing can be this good." But if they
stay around long enough, get to know enough people, hear
enough of their stories, and find out the real source of their
power, they are very likely to change their minds about the
church.

This book is written first of all for those who are disciples of
Jesus Christ to help us appreciate God's plan for the church and
to heed his direction about how to make her glorious. God has
cried enough. It is time for the church to want to please him in
every way and for the church to have the impact he designed her
to have. Absolutely nothing else can make the difference in the

world that the glorious church of Jesus Christ can make.

Second, this book is for the seeker. It is for the person who has nothing positive to say about the word "church." It is to introduce you to a whole new world. And hear this: Each person who writes in this volume writes out of rich experience with the biblical church in our modern world. Listen closely and you will see this. We are not from a sinless church, but we are from a church that has learned from Jesus how to keep dealing with sin. We are not from a perfect church, but we are from a church that has found the grace of God that enables us to strive to learn new things day after day.

We are all humbled to have ended up in such a community, such a family, and such a people. We don't think for a minute that we deserve it or that our intelligence or hard work made it happen. It is a gift of God. When we see what is happening in our own local fellowship and, at the same time, how the message of Jesus is linking us in thought, in love and in action with fellow disciples in congregations all over the globe, we stand in awe and say truly there is *glory in the church!*

※

And now some practical words to help you get the most out of this study: The book is divided into three sections. In Part I— "Born in Eternity"—we will look at the divine origins of the church. If we are to appreciate the meaning of the true church, we must understand that it is not the creation of man but the work of God. Until we grasp this we will never have the undying loyalty to the church that every disciple must have. In Part II— "Designed for Impact"—we will look at some of the principles revealed in the New Testament that make the church a unique and powerful instrument for God. And finally in Part III— "Directed to Love"—we will explore the heart of the church, our relationships in Christ, which are so different from the relationships we experience in the world. Many of you will quickly recognize that the chapter titles here come from the "one another" passages, scriptures crucial to understanding the unique relationships that Christians are to have. So few "church" members have experienced what these passages describe; they have missed the glorious way God works to encourage us, challenge us and mature us.

At the end of each selection, you will find questions to help you take what you are reading and put it right in the center of your life. Wrestle with these. Share your responses and conclusions with others. We are not called to just admire the church but to live in it and to become, ourselves, part of the glory. So be grateful, be inspired and make some decisions that will change the world. God has cried enough.

T.A.J.

PART I

Born in Eternity

The church of Jesus Christ is not of human origin. It was divinely predicted, divinely established, and it continues to be divinely loved and led. The church will succeed in its divine mission because the church is from God.

1 Foreseen by Prophets

G. STEVE KINNARD
New York City, New York

The word that Isaiah son of Amoz saw concerning Judah and
Jerusalem.

In days to come
>   the mountain of the LORD's house
shall be established as the highest of the mountains,
>   and shall be raised above the hills;
all the nations shall stream to it.
Many peoples shall come and say,
>   "Come, let us go up to the mountain of the LORD,
>   to the house of the God of Jacob;
that he may teach us his ways
>   and that we may walk in his paths."
For out of Zion shall go forth instruction,
and the word of the LORD from Jerusalem.

Isaiah 2:1-4[1]

One of the greatest speeches of the twentieth century was
given before a multitude assembled in Washington, D.C. on
August 28,1963. In what we now call the "I Have A Dream"
speech, Dr. Martin Luther King, Jr. captured the ideals of the
American civil rights movement. In perhaps the most famous
lines from that message, he said, "I have a dream that my four
little children will one day live in a nation where they
will not be judged by the color of their skin but by the content
of their character; I have a dream today." Throughout his
speech, King echoed the voices of the biblical prophets and
called upon the images they had used to portray his dream of
racial equality.

These prophets of Israel had God's dreams placed on their
hearts. Through inspiration, they saw things that others simply
could not see. They saw what would truly be "a new world
order," a new community and a deeper fellowship. Through

---

[1] *The New Revised Standard Version* (Nashville, Tennessee: Thomas Nelson Publishers, 1989).

God's power and the spirit of revelation, they broke free of a narrow nationalism and envisioned a worldwide family of believers united by a fresh, new relationship with God. Although you never hear the word "church" from the Old Testament prophets, they clearly saw it coming and painted vivid pictures that would be fulfilled dramatically in the first century by Jesus, the apostles and the earliest disciples.

The Church in Prophecy

The Bible contains many specific prophecies about Christ and his beloved, the church, demonstrating that for generations God had the church on his heart and mind. He was waiting for the exact, perfect moment to unleash the glory of his spiritual kingdom in the world.

Before time began, God planned a way to draw humanity to him. Genesis 3:15 may be one of the first clues to his intention. He prophesied that the seed of woman would crush the head of the serpent, the first prophecy about the cross of Jesus. The seed which crushed Satan's head, Jesus, also became the foundation stone of the church.

Isaiah 2:1-4, quoted above, shows clearly that the coming "mountain of the Lord's house"—the church, the kingdom of God on earth (see Hebrews 12:18-23)—would be established in Jerusalem but made up of all nations. The church would be an international fellowship bridging racial extremes, social differences and economic boundaries. Even on the first day of its existence, as we read about it in Acts 2, we see the words of Isaiah being fulfilled. Men and women from all over the world streamed into the church and enjoyed a most uncommon fellowship. In Isaiah 11:6-9, the prophet again described the coming kingdom, saying it would bring natural enemies together. When Jesus came and led Jew and Gentile, slave and free, barbarian and Scythian into his church (Colossians 3:11), Isaiah's dream was fulfilled.

Joel 2:28-32 tells us of a great outpouring of the Spirit that would lead to people being saved—again, in Jerusalem. On the day of Pentecost, Peter called attention to God's miracles which were evident for all to see, and he cited the fulfillment of this passage to begin his famed sermon that led to the conversion of the 3,000 and the establishment of the church.

In Daniel 2:36-44, God gave a timetable for when the kingdom would come. A simple analysis of history reveals that the "fourth kingdom" (v40) was the Roman Empire and "during the time of those kings" (v44) refers to the Caesars of Rome. True to God's plan, this prophecy was fulfilled by the establishment of Jesus' church during the days of the Roman Empire, which has been in ruins for years—unlike God's everlasting kingdom, the church.

Blessed Are the Eyes That See

Before time began, God planned to build his church. Like a careful architect, he drew up the plans detail by detail. He recorded these details for us to explore. We don't have to guess what the church should be like. We can see the blueprints laid out across the pages of the Bible. We need to check the church we were brought up in against God's blueprint. If we know very little about the church of Jesus, it's all in the Bible for our discovering.

A number of years ago, I started a club based upon the movie *Dead Poets Society.* My club was called the "Dead Apostles Society." On occasion, a few of my friends and I would gather to read our favorite scriptures to each other. We began each meeting by reading Luke 10:23-24:

> Then he turned to his disciples and said privately, "Blessed are the eyes that see what you see. For I tell you that many prophets and kings wanted to see what you see but did not see it, and to hear what you hear but did not hear it."

As we continue this study of God's church, this verse should ring in our ears. We are seeing and hearing things that the great kings and prophets of the Old Testament longed to see and hear. King David would love to be in your place right now. Jeremiah would gladly trade places with you. Isaiah, Solomon, Micah, Hezekiah, Daniel, Josiah—marvel at the fact that they all would have loved to know what you know.

LIFE APPLICATION

How does it make you feel to know that God was working to establish his kingdom on earth centuries before it came into existence? What difference does it make to you to be part of the culmination of such a great plan?

In awe of Gods power and his plan. Privileged to be part of it + called to fulfill my purpose within it.

Read again Luke 10:23-24. How blessed do you believe you are?

I believe I am blessed in everyway but dont always feel that daily. I need to meditate on the great gift I have been given

God's kingdom should include all people. What excites you the most about the diversity of the church and the fact that it is a worldwide movement?

I love that in just a short time (10 yrs since I came) the church has grown radically all over the world & that I personally know disciples all over the world.

God dreams about his kingdom. What are your dreams for God's kingdom?

I dream for the church to continue to grow radically, to plant a church in every city over 100,000 by 2000. and for me personally to strive to grow & be used fully by God according to his plan.

2 Built by Jesus

Tom A. Jones
Tuscaloosa, Alabama

> "But what about you?" he asked. "Who do you say I am?"
> Simon Peter answered, "You are the Christ, the Son of the living God."
> Jesus replied, "Blessed are you, Simon son of Jonah, for this was not revealed to you by man, but by my Father in heaven. And I tell you that you are Peter, and on this rock I will build my church, and the gates of Hades will not overcome it."
> Matthew 16:15-18

Disciples of Jesus are people who have decided that what is important to Jesus is going to be important to them. There can be no doubt from this passage what is important to Jesus. These words were spoken by him at what may very well have been the crucial hinge point in his ministry. After spending months with those he had chosen, he took them on a rare trip to the area around Caesarea Philippi—twenty-five miles north of the Sea of Galilee. Jesus apparently wanted a quieter setting, removed from the Jewish crowds, where he could confront his followers with the most important question of all: "Who do you say that I am?" (Matthew 16:15).

There, in the shadow of a great temple built by Herod the Great to honor Caesar, and with temples to pagan Syrian gods dotting the surrounding countryside, Peter stated the supreme truth: *"You are the Christ, the Son of the living God."*

"My Church"

Jesus affirmed Peter's confession, announcing that it was a conclusion inspired by God himself. But, as best we can tell, the disciples then heard from Jesus a phrase they had never heard before: *"my church."* "Yes, Peter, I am the Son of God," said Jesus, "and on this bedrock truth I am going to build my church." The word for "church" in the Greek text is the word *ekklesia* and means literally "the called out." Today the word "church" sounds religious to all who hear it, but the word *ekklesia* (which could be translated "assembly," "congregation," "people," or in some contexts by a more modern word— "team") had no particular religious meaning. The word simply referred to a group of people gathered for some purpose. (It is even used in Acts 19:32 and 41 to refer to a pagan mob furious over the impact of Christian evangelism in their city.)

What is unique and important about Jesus' statement is not the word "church" but the phrase "my church." There were thousands of "churches": hundreds of groups in the world with agendas, teachings and plans. Many of those were represented in a cosmopolitan region like that of Caesarea Philippi. But there was only one Son of God, and he was going to build his singularly unique group, his people, his team, his family, his army.

This last word, "army," seems particularly appropriate in view of the imagery Jesus employs as he goes on to describe the activity of his people. Once his group is together, built and established on the solid rock of his divine nature, "the gates of Hades will not overcome it," or as the Revised Standard Version has it, "will not prevail against it." As a child listening to sermons based on this statement, I imagined the church as a walled city that sat waiting for the attacks of Satan. Like many people I had a case of theological dyslexia. What I saw with my mind's eye was backwards.

In Jesus' image, the church is the advancing and conquering army, not the passive walled city. Ever on the offensive, the church will encounter resistance, but never be stopped by it. Whenever an ancient army attacked a city, it would always concentrate on *the gates* for they were the most vulnerable. The church will go after the very "gates of Hades" ("the powers of death" RSV), and while disciples will die for their faith, the church will march on because she belongs to the Son of God who himself faced the gates of death and rose in triumph.

What Is Important to Jesus

At the most crucial of times in his work with his disciples, Jesus took Peter's confession and immediately tied it to the building of his church. There are some powerful lessons here for us:

First, the church is important to Jesus, and she must be just as important to us. It may be easier to love and be loyal to Jesus than to the church. He is perfect; his church is not. But he loves his church and sacrificed to build her into a glorious body. We must do no less. A person can work for an employer and not agree with him on what is important. A person can live under a president's rule and disagree with him on what is important. But we cannot call Jesus "Lord" unless what is important to Jesus becomes important to us. That is the nature of lordship and the nature of discipleship.

Whenever someone loves my wife or one of my children, I feel in a very real way that they are loving me. Hurt my family; you hurt me. Love my family; you love me. Jesus feels no differently about his church. Hurt his church; you hurt him. Love his church; you love him.

Second, a right understanding of Jesus always leads to the church. If your thinking is biblical, you simply cannot talk very long about Jesus without talking about his church. You cannot have one without the other. Other New Testament passages describing Jesus as the head and the church as the body make that connection absolutely clear. The work Jesus began was to be carried on, and there was only one plan: the church. God sent his Son into this world, not just to amaze us, but to unite us into a group that would keep leaving his imprint on the world.

Here is why the articles in this book are so important: The church is no ordinary group. It is the only one Jesus ever started. It is the only one with his mission. It is the only one that will be saved. It is *his* church. We must love her, thank God for her, study about her, support her, pray for her, sacrifice for her and do all we can to make her all Jesus wanted her to be.

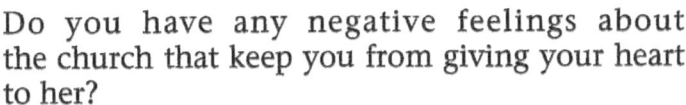
LIFE APPLICATION

Do you have any negative feelings about the church that keep you from giving your heart to her?

How does your attitude toward the church need to change in order to line up with Jesus' attitude?

How do you think your attitude toward the church affects what the church becomes in your city or town?

Given Jesus' teaching in Matthew 16, what is going to be the final outcome of the church? How does that need to affect your thinking?

3 Bought at a Price

McKenney, Texas

Do you not know that your body is a temple of the Holy Spirit, who is in you, whom you have received from God? You are not your own; you were bought at a price. Therefore honor God with your body.

1 Corinthians 6:19-20

Keep watch over yourselves and all the flock of which the Holy Spirit has made you overseers. Be shepherds of the church of God, which he bought with his own blood.

Acts 20:28

The church of Jesus Christ has great value. She was bought at an enormous price. Her very existence came as the result of a costly sacrifice—the death of Jesus Christ on Calvary's hill. That event was no afterthought in the mind of God, nor was it even an idea conceived in response to man's sinful fall in the Garden of Eden. According to 1 Peter 1:20, Jesus was chosen for this task "before the creation of the world." Revelation 13:8 tells us that he was "slain from the creation of the world." This truth contains one of the most amazing concepts in all the Bible!

We decide to have children with the firm hope that they will turn out well, live meaningful lives and end up in heaven with God. If we desired to have six children, but knew in advance that all but one of them would reject us and our teaching in their lives, we likely would change our minds about having children. The pain would be too great even to contemplate.

He Paid a Debt He Did Not Owe

God created a world in which human beings are free moral agents, able to choose right or wrong. Possessing all knowledge, he knew the full extent to which we humans would rebel in that freedom of choice and reject him in the process. Yet, his desire to pour his love into a relationship with us led him to continue

22

with his creative process in spite of the pain his creatures would cause him. Is that realization not staggering to you?

The love of God is no ordinary love nor is the interest of Jesus any ordinary interest. God is so committed to mankind that *no* price was too high to pay for a relationship with us. *Unbelievable!* God became a man, suffered and died on a cross to redeem and adopt the "few" who would choose the narrow road. As the words of the devotional song put it, "He paid a debt he did not owe; I owed a debt I could not pay." The pain suffered by God and his Son at the crucifixion was great. Evidently, the value of a saved church is greater. In the sentiments of John 12:25, Jesus *hated* his life in order to bless our lives. He gave up his life in order to give life to his church—his people, his friends.

The price Jesus paid involved a sacrificial love which did not flinch at the thought of leaving heaven to become a despised man and face a brutal death as a common criminal. More amazingly, that divine love did not recoil at the idea of being rejected by the large majority of the ones for whom he died. No wonder Paul wrote, "Thanks be to God for his indescribable gift!" (2 Corinthians 9:15). Man gives love in hopes of prompting a returned love. He may continue to give love when a loving response does not immediately ensue. But to continually give love in the face of indifferent or *hateful* rejection is almost unheard of in humans. However, anything *less* is unheard of in God's overtures to us!

His Price Must Set Our Values

The price God paid for the church clearly established our value to him. We do not pay a higher price for an object than it is worth to us, and neither did God. But the price paid must do more than determine our value to God; it must also set our own values in life. If God was willing to go to the greatest lengths possible to redeem us, then we must see the implications for our own lives. After all, we are to be "imitators of God" as "dearly loved children" (Ephesians 5:1).

One implication that is readily apparent is the value the church must hold to each of us. Many years ago, this little phrase was repeated among people who valued spirituality but disdained organized religion: "Up with Christ, down with the church!" All they knew of church was what they saw in traditional religion, and they rightly rejected it. But, sad to say, they did not see the church as God designed it to be—his very blood-bought family! To exalt Christ is to exalt the church, for he is the head of it (Ephesians 1:22-23). Let us treasure the church the way God does, and let our love for it be seen in our attitudes and speech. May God never see in our hearts attitudes toward the church which are negative, and may man never hear from our mouths words which demean it!

Another important lesson gained from God's love for the church is that sacrifice is a continual part of the price we pay to be in it. His love drove him to hold back nothing, and our love must move us to do the same. Our focus must not be on what the church can do for us, but rather what we can sacrifice for the church. In God's Old Testament family, the nation of Israel, sacrifices were limited in time, cost and obligation. When an animal was offered, the price was paid in time and money, and then the obligation was fulfilled. In God's New Testament family, the church, our sacrifice is a living one of the seven-days-per-week-twenty-four-hours-per-day variety (Romans 12:1-2).

A final implication regarding our view of the church is that our love, like God's, must be unconditional. He loves the church in spite of the human frailty inherent in it. The church at Corinth was replete with serious problems, and yet God was determined to bring them to victory. "He will keep you strong to the end, so that you will be blameless on the day of our Lord Jesus Christ" (1 Corinthians 1:8). How do you see imperfections in the church—as an opportunity to love unconditionally or to criticize? If we expect God to love us with all our blemishes, we had better open our hearts to love his family in exactly the same way. As James put it, "Judgment without mercy will be shown to anyone who has not been merciful. Mercy triumphs over judgment!" (James 2:13). And Peter wrote: "Above all, love each other deeply, because love covers over a multitude of sins" (1 Peter 4:8). Let's think, feel and live as those *bought at a price!*

LIFE APPLICATION

Is the idea of no longer belonging to yourself a positive or a negative idea to you? Why?

Does being bought at a price make you grateful on a consistent, sustained basis? (Ask those who know you best how grateful a person you seem to be.)

How do you feel, knowing that God was (and still is) willing to suffer the pain of rejection by the majority of his creatures in order to have a relationship with you? (Write out these feelings and try to get in touch with your true views of God and the Christian life.)

How highly do you value the church? Make a list of the good points and bad points you see in it, and then think and pray through your overall attitudes and responses to these things.

4 Led by the Savior

RUSS EWELL
San Francisco, California

He is the image of the invisible God, the firstborn over all creation. For by him all things were created: things in heaven and on earth, visible and invisible, whether thrones or powers or rulers or authorities; all things were created by him and for him. He is before all things, and in him all things hold together. And he is the head of the body, the church; he is the beginning and the firstborn from among the dead, so that in everything he might have the supremacy. For God was pleased to have all his fullness dwell in him, and through him to reconcile to himself all things, whether things on earth or things in heaven, by making peace through his blood, shed on the cross.

Colossians 1:15-20

There is nothing that can be achieved without leadership. We can talk about principles, policies and right thinking, the fundamentals of leadership, but when those discussions are finished, this remains: the essential ability of a few individuals to chart an inspiring course of action! This world will be influenced and changed by the group which has the best leadership.

In history's cavalcade of leadership there is one who stands above them all. In him was the perfect blend of all strengths, unimpaired by weakness. This man was Jesus. It is his life that beckons us to follow and imitate. The best leaders of men will not be those who pioneer a humanistic effort sustained by earthbound motives; they will be those who emulate the timeless life of Jesus. Their leadership will simply be a reflection (2 Corinthians 3:18) of this special and powerful life, and this group will be the one that seizes the day. Two thousand years after it began, the church of Christ is alive and well because she is *of Christ* and it is Christ who leads her.

Deep in every culture, nation and individual heart, there is a need for leadership. Sadly, negative experiences have created a general disillusionment and distrust of leaders in the hearts of most people. This problem is obvious in the world, but it can also be brought into the church, unless we remember who is truly leading.

No Leader Like Jesus

Paul wrote the words to the Colossians that open this article to remind disciples of the uniqueness of Jesus and the fact that he is central to this great kingdom of ours. Look carefully at the one who leads us, and be encouraged and inspired.

He is the image of the invisible God. No man walking the earth has ever led like Jesus. Jesus is God. His leadership is flawless. When we keep ourselves, our churches and this great kingdom focused on Jesus, then he will be our leader; and we will be assured victory in the saving of lost souls. Thrones, powers and authorities will not overthrow or defeat him for he is greater than all these. How can we worry when we are led by the Lord and Savior?

Paul speaks of Jesus being the source of unity that holds all things together. The unity of the church is a sure sign that Jesus is leading. When we see all races, backgrounds, nations and cultures together, this can only be the fruit of the leadership of Jesus. It is our responsibility to listen closely to Jesus and build the kingdom of God as he directs so that all men may see our unity and have the opportunity to come to him.

Focused on Jesus

In opening the letter to the Colossians (1:1-6) Paul says he has heard about the Colossians' faith in Jesus. I find that arresting! There are too many of us who are more inspired by men than by Jesus, and as a consequence, our faith is misplaced. We lose courage whenever those men cannot be there for us, or when they sin and make mistakes. Often we are not led by Jesus but by the strength of men who are weighed down by the pressure we put on them to be Jesus for us. Put your faith in Jesus, and then great things will happen for you.

The late George Gurganus and I were part of the ministry staff meetings led by Kip McKean in the late 1980s. During the breaks George and I would frequently get time to talk. On one occasion, I asked this brother, more than forty years my senior, what he thought made Kip so different. Still a young leader, I was trying to understand why Kip was chosen by God to have such huge impact, beyond other men of great talent and desire. I will never forget George's response. He said, "I have never seen anyone more devoted and determined to be like Jesus than Kip." He went on to talk about Kip's commitment to follow the plan and fulfill the dream of Jesus. I now see this as the quality that the Colossian church was called to, by Paul, in Colossians 1:10. Paul told them to focus on pleasing Jesus. God works through Kip to lead powerfully in this modern age because he is so clearly focused on letting Jesus be his leader. May we all be so focused.

With the Vision of Jesus

Colossians 1:24 through 2:5 describes the heart and vision of Paul. He tells us that he proclaims Jesus and works with the energy of the Holy Spirit, to present everyone perfect in Christ. The person who is led by Jesus is not only consumed with pleasing him and being like him, but also with calling others to imitate his life. He looks at each person with vision and hope for what they can become, not with despair over who they are. If we are to help God's kingdom spread worldwide, we must be visionaries who see our neighborhoods, cities and nations filled with disciples. We must learn to look at everyone the way Jesus would look at them, with the conviction that by the power of God they can change and make a difference in the world.

Jesus will lead his church to victory. He will not fail. He never does. But will we follow and share in the victory?

LIFE APPLICATION

Would others say of you: "He/she just cannot get enough of Jesus?" How do others see you seeking more and more in your relationship with Jesus?

Why do you stay in the kingdom? Does this mean you will be here forever?

Do you find that you are consumed with negative attitudes toward Christians and leaders? Could it be because you are not focused on the Savior?

In your discipling of others, what do you do to get them focused on Jesus? What can you do to make this more of a strength in your work with people?

5 Loved As a Wife

KAY MCKEAN
Kihei, Hawaii

Husbands, love your wives, just as Christ loved the church and gave himself up for her...to present her to himself as a radiant church...holy and blameless. In this same way, husbands ought to love their wives as their own bodies. He who loves his wife loves himself. After all, no one ever hated his own body, but he feeds and cares for it, just as Christ does the church....This is a profound mystery—but I am talking about Christ and the church....

Ephesians 5:25-33

"I love you, honey,....it's just that I'm not ready for that kind of commitment. I want a relationship with you, but I'm just not the marrying kind." Throughout romantic history men have made this statement, and women have shed tears over it. We can acknowledge that the statement is ludicrous, because if a man really loves a woman, he wants to be committed to her, to marry her, and to be with her forever.

Yet, many people who would feel disdain at a statement like this might be the first to announce something equally as ludicrous: *"I love Jesus,....it's just that I don't want to be committed to the church. I want a relationship with God but I'm just not the churchgoing kind."* Men and women alike have often failed to understand the importance of marriage and of the church in the eyes of God. Both have been trivialized by those who say they aren't necessary or are out of date. But Ephesians 5 clearly shows us God's intentions for both the marriage relationship and the church.

An Endangered Institution

Marriage today is an endangered institution. When half of all marriages end in divorce, when couples opt to just live together, when celebrities talk unashamedly of multiple marriage breakups, we can see why people are afraid to head for the altar. But lest we think this is a modern phenomenon, it's important to realize that marriage was often not held in high esteem by the Roman or even the Jewish world. Contrary to what we may think, the first century was not the "good old days" for husbands and wives!

Then along came the apostle Paul, who delivered a radical message: *Husbands, be like Jesus! Sacrifice for your wife! Bring out the best qualities she has! Care for her, protect her, love her!* It makes me smile to think of Paul as such a romantic! He truly saw marriage at its best, the way God intended it to be. Then, he used this relationship as a metaphor for Christ and his relationship with the church.

Christ Loves the Church

Perhaps the most moving stories are those in which someone gives up his or her life for a loved one. This is the kind of love we see exhibited in Christ as he died for each of us, for his church. How can anyone believe that the church is unimportant when Jesus died on the cross for her? Christ had a plan for his people, and for that plan to succeed he had to go through the torture of the cross. I love the church because Jesus loves the church, because he died for the church. If I am to follow Jesus, I will give my life for the church as well.

He Presents Her As Radiant

People have said there is no such thing as an ugly bride. A woman walking down the aisle to meet the man who loves her is a beauty indeed. Because of his love for her, she radiates life and hope and happiness. Christ's desire is that the church be beautiful and radiant in this world. Because of his love for us, he sees us, the church, as a thing of beauty. Our love, our service, our commitment, our conviction make us stand out. My desire is to do my part to make the church blameless in this world, in order that the church can make Jesus proud of his "bride."

He Feeds and Cares for Her

Christ consistently meets the church's every need. We have solid food—the word of God. We have leaders to guide us and friends to support us. We have the assurance of forgiveness and the promise of eternal life. At times, just as an ungrateful wife sees only the negatives about her husband, people in the church can be too focused on problems or needs, and lose sight of their blessings. Jesus is the good "husband" who provides the church with "one blessing after another" (John 1:16).

Worthy of Our Trust

A good husband is a rare find in this world. I am grateful that I happen to have one! I am married to a man who loves God and who loves me, and for that I feel incredibly blessed. Through our nearly two decades of marriage, I have seen Randy sacrifice for me, challenge me to be my best, and take care of me through times of sickness, moodiness, childbearing and child-raising. His commitment and love for me have pulled me through many a difficult time, and thanks to him, and the grace of God, I can stand as a faithful disciple today. He has proven worthy of a wife's trust, and it is a joy to be able to love him, submit to him, and to go through life together with him.

More than any earthly husband, our Lord Jesus has proven himself worthy of our trust. Christ is our example; he loves us with a tender and enduring love. As a church, we look to him for love, care, protection, knowing that as we submit to Christ and serve him, we will be the church he wants us to be. Just as a joyful and radiant wife brings honor to her husband, we as the church must bring honor to Christ. We are the shining bride of Christ, we are the church, we are his true love. He is forever committed to us—in sickness and in health, for richer or for poorer, for better or for worse. And what God has joined together, no thing and no one has the power to separate; even death will not break this marriage bond!

LIFE APPLICATION

Have you ever thought that loving Jesus is easier than loving the church? Why is it so important to love the church with all your heart?

How does it affect you to think of Jesus being committed to you as a loving husband is committed to his wife?

How do you desire to grow spiritually in order to help the church bring honor to Jesus?

What commitment do you personally make to the other members of Christ's church?

6 Sent into the World

Dallas, Texas

"As you have sent me into the world, I have sent them into the world."

John 17:18

The church is here for a reason. She has a clearly defined and clearly divine mission. In John 17, Jesus prayed for his apostles whom he was sending into the world and for all the people who would become Christians through their message. In Acts 1:8, Jesus told them to take the message to the ends of the earth. In the KJV, the word used here is "uttermost" (or "the farthest"). It is my conviction that we will reach the uttermost parts of the world only if all parts of the church, from the top leaders to the "uttermost" parts of the body, are sent into the world. In the book of Acts, we see the whole church functioning as one unit. Though "they," the church, numbered in the thousands, all of them had the same purpose and commitment (Acts 2:42-47, 4:32-34).

The Conviction

Jesus had great conviction that he had been sent into the world. When his disciples first began to follow him, he told them, "Let us go somewhere else—to the nearby villages—so I can preach there also. That is why I have come" (Mark 1:38). Jesus not only *lived* his conviction of bringing people to God— he *died* for it. Truly, by his wounds we have been healed (1 Peter 2:24).

The church in the first century clearly understood that they were sent into the world. In Acts 2:47, we see that the great Jerusalem church was making disciples every day. Their conviction then spread to the others, so that even years later we see the Gentile churches growing daily (Acts 16:5). Every Christian, be it an apostle or an ordinary disciple, a Jew or Gentile, had the conviction to spread the Word.

As disciples, our conviction is that Jesus came to bring people to God. It's easy to have the conviction that the first-century church was sent into the world. But we must now have conviction that, as Jesus' church today, we, too, are being sent into the world. The true church will do many good things, but her top priority will always be to evangelize this world.

Remember Paul's use of the head and body analogy in Colossians 1:18 and Ephesians 1:22-23? We are Jesus' body! He is the head. It's that simple. The head directs the body. If the head tells the body to eat breakfast, the body obeys! If Christ is the decision maker, then he should be deciding what his body's purpose will be. If Jesus is truly the head of our church, we should see it reflected in the common purpose of the members.

The Bible also commands that we imitate Jesus if we claim to live in him (1 John 2:6). We cannot really be following Jesus without imitating his love for people. Since Jesus desires that all men come to a knowledge of the truth and be saved (1 Timothy 2:4), so we, too, must love everyone and yearn for them to know God and to go to heaven.

When I think of disciples with this conviction, I think of my parents. Earlier this year, they heard about a mission team being sent to their hometown. As my father and I spoke on the phone, one week shy of his 70th birthday, he told me he wanted to go. After he hung up, he told my mother to start packing for India. Two hours later my father died of an asthma attack. I was sad he died, but I know that he died with conviction about being sent into the world. Two days after the funeral, my mother decided to go out evangelizing to keep herself from falling into self-pity. That day she met a woman who became a Christian! My mother decided to go on the mission team without my dad. After arriving in India, she met another person who became a Christian. She has a conviction about her purpose, because she knows that God has sent his church into the world.

The Confidence

Jesus was not only full of conviction about his purpose, he was confident of being sent *by God*—he says so, more than twenty times in the book of John. As his body, we must be confident about being sent *by God* into the world. We must see our workplace, our school, our neighborhood, our fitness center, our children's sports team and our extended family as our mission fields. Maybe you have been asked to start a new Bible discussion group or even to help plant a church. If God wants to send you, be confident! Perhaps you became a disciple in a foreign country. In all likelihood, God wants to send you back to your own people where you will be more effective.

Sometimes we even hear leaders confessing they are insecure. Since the word "insecure" is not found in the Bible, what they are really saying is they are fearful and faithless. Who wants to follow an "insecure" leader who doubts he is sent by God? Where would the kingdom be if all the leaders were like that? Such a leader needs to make a decision to repent and be confident.

It does not matter what your age is, how good your health is, how talented you are or what your role is—you should be confident that you are sent by God into the world.

With the earth's population at five billion lost souls, the church must be consumed with "being sent" into the world. Going into the world cannot be a "nice hobby" or a "church activity." It must be the very center of our dreams, our goals and our lives. This will only be a reality if every member of the body, down to the very last "part," has the conviction and the confidence that the church has been sent by God into the world.

LIFE APPLICATION

Why is so important to understand that going into the world with the message of Jesus is a mission from God?

Do you really believe that you are just as chosen and sent by God as your leaders?

Does every member of your ministry group have the same conviction about being sent into the world? Regardless of your role, what can you do to make a difference?

What situations make you "insecure," i.e. fearful and faithless, in carrying out your mission? Is God able to help you with these? Is he capable of giving you a victory?

PART II

Designed
for
Impact

*God established his church in a
needy world so that a difference would be
made in thousands, even millions, of lives.
The New Testament shows us those qualities
that will make the church distinctive and
powerful in a world crying out for help.*

7 Where Truth Really Matters

RICK MAULE
Melbourne Beach, Florida

> Although I hope to come to you soon, I am writing you these instructions so that, if I am delayed, you will know how people ought to conduct themselves in God's household, which is the church of the living God, the pillar and foundation of the truth.
>
> 1 Timothy 3:14-15

It was something like a wrestling match. Every time we studied the Bible with Bill and Diana it was a tense, twisting battle over facts, words and doctrines. We were concerned that they find the truth and not base their lives on human religious traditions, but they struggled with the truth that we tried to bring to them. They had visited our congregation after having been "burned" by negative experiences in a number of denominational churches in Charlotte. They had even worked for a famous televangelist couple when a scandal was uncovered in the late 1980s.

Mary Nell and I fell in love with these people, and we were thrilled as step by step their lives started changing! But these folks not only studied their Bibles closely, they put the church under a microscope.

From Matthew 7:24 we know that God's truth should be the "rock" on which our lives are built, but here in 1 Timothy 3:15 we find that the church is "the pillar and foundation of the truth." It's like God is saying, "The church depends on the truth, but the truth also depends on the church." To put it another way, God's church is supposed to provide a solid dwelling place for truth, a household where there is no deceit and where things are called what they are. The church grows only if it is willing to continue fearlessly "speaking the truth in love" (Ephesians 4:15).

Bill and Diana were attracted to the loving honesty they encountered in studying the Word with true disciples. Probably because of their painful religious past, these dedicated "Bereans" watched everything we said and did to see if it matched up with the Scriptures. Were we really different from the denominations they had left before?

As the studies progressed, I sensed that some sort of test for Bill and Diana was about to come, and come it did. After we returned from a leadership conference in Johannesburg, South Africa, we were fired up and ready to turn our city upside down. I planned a special midweek sermon that would convict the church, and at the same time, inspire Bill and Diana with something so powerful, so radical, that they would just have to become disciples! Then my phone started ringing.

First, the church administrator called to tell me that a number of our members had recently bounced contribution checks. Frustrated, I thought, "I'll have to hit this strongly in the announcements."

Then one of the zone leaders called, informing me that a woman in the church had been charged with stealing over a thousand dollars from her employer (who was also a disciple). "We will have to deal decisively with this, but maybe we can do it in her small group," I reasoned. This kind of news would likely be a real "downer" for the whole church. And who knows what effect it would have on Bill and Diana?

Then the third call came. One of our interns was on the line to report that one of our group leaders, who was also our main song leader, had been caught in a major financial deception involving thousands of dollars in stolen rent money. There was no way to avoid it now! It couldn't wait. All this would have to be brought before the Lord, the church...and Bill and Diana. How would they react to yet another church scandal? Would their newly found zeal for the kingdom turn sour? Would their skepticism be confirmed? Would they grab their Bibles and run? My Johannesburg message would have to wait.

Speaking the Truth

That Wednesday night I addressed the sins of the church head on. We talked specifically and truthfully about the problems that had come into the light. I challenged the congregation to have godly fear and absolute integrity in financial matters. It did not escape my attention that Bill and Diana were present.

The church was visibly sobered. Many were convicted and repentant, and went out of their way to thank me for saying what needed to be said. Then as I hugged one of the brothers, I looked over his shoulder, and my eyes met Bill's. I walked over and hugged him. Then I asked what he thought about the service. Although my question sounded casual, I knew a lot was on the line. Would he be angry? Disappointed? Disillusioned that the glorious kingdom he had found was less than perfect? My heart relaxed as he warmly welcomed my hug. Looking into my eyes he responded, "I thought it was incredible! I've never been part of a church where this kind of thing was dealt with so honestly and directly!" As it turned out, it was our willingness to tell the truth—the sometimes ugly and painful truth—that helped these seekers to find God's church.

I'm happy to say that today Bill and Diana are both disciples. They love God and his kingdom! The two disciples whose sin was exposed that night have repented and made restitution and are doing well spiritually. The congregation now has strong convictions about financial righteousness, and the church is growing!

The church will always be under the scrutiny of outsiders and enemies who "refuse to love the truth and so be saved" (2 Thessalonians 2:10) but also by open-hearted seekers who are "on the side of truth" (John 18:37). As "the pillar and foundation of the truth," God's church must always resist the temptation to promote and defend ourselves with the "worldly weapons" of slick words and deceit (2 Corinthians 10:4). We must never smooth over the sharp edges of the raw truth, whether it be in God's word or in our lives. We must never cloak the faults of the church by putting a positive spin on our failures and sins. Our best defense will always be the truth.

LIFE APPLICATION

What happens to the church when it stops having a passion for truth?

Speaking the truth as it is found in God's word and speaking the truth about our failures and sins often represents two different stories. Why must the church of Jesus Christ be as committed to the second as to the first?

If you see the church backing away from commitment to the truth in any way, what will you do? What will be your heart and your prayer?

Telling the truth can often be painful. What rationalizations or excuses do we as disciples use to avoid telling the truth about ourselves and others?

8 Where Silence Is Not an Option

Doug Webber
Los Angeles, California

It is written: "I believed; therefore I have spoken." With that same spirit of faith we also believe and therefore speak....
2 Corinthians 4:13

"What do you think about the death penalty?" "Should sex education be a required course in our schools?" "Do you believe that the Bible is the Word of God?" "I'm conducting a survey to find out how people feel about...." "Please call this phone number and answer yes or no as to whether...."

We live in a society where people's opinions and beliefs concerning a variety of issues are often sought. People quickly discover that it is acceptable to be "undecided" or "not sure" and can quickly find peace in offering these responses. They also discover that it is equally acceptable to exercise their right not to voice any opinion or stance. People often find it more comfortable to deal with the more controversial issues, like religion, in this way. Typically people have not made the necessary effort or taken adequate time to be more than "undecided" or "not sure" or they fear the consequences that come from taking a strong stance (John 12:42-43; Psalm 78:9).

Boldly Speak

Those who do speak out and voice their spiritual beliefs often weigh their words very carefully so as to not express too much conviction. Statements such as "For me, I believe..." are not uncommon and are often the words of those too cowardly to proclaim God's truth. But the church of Jesus Christ is in the speaking business. We believe, and therefore we must speak. John F. Kennedy once said that "the hottest places in hell are reserved for those who, in a time of moral crisis, choose to preserve their neutrality!" Disciples of Jesus who make up his church simply must speak. They must confidently and unashamedly proclaim the life-giving message of the gospel to those who like it and those who do not (Romans 1:16-17).

Speaking is important to God. He *spoke* the world into existence.

> And God *said*, "Let there be light," and there was light.... And God *said*, "Let the water under the sky be gathered to one place, and let dry ground appear." And it was so.... And God *said*, "Let the land produce living creatures according to their kinds: livestock, creatures that move along the ground, and wild animals, each according to its kind." And it was so (Genesis 1:3, 9, 24, emphasis added).

Not only was the spoken word of God involved in creation, but it continues to be involved in the *new* creation. We, as part of God's original creation, have become part of God's new creation as disciples (2 Corinthians 5:17), and this spiritual transformation has come about because someone was not silent.

> And you also were included in Christ when you *heard* the word of truth, the gospel of your salvation. Having believed, you were marked in him with a seal, the promised Holy Spirit... (Ephesians 1:13, emphasis added).

Individuals who confidently speak God's truth to others have discovered the power to truly change the lives and eternal destinies of people. Though this power ultimately is from God, it cannot be made available to those who desperately need it if those to whom it has been entrusted (the church) are not speaking the truth. It's exciting to know that we in the church not only *must be* but *get to be* spokesmen and spokeswomen for God.

> His intent was that now, through the church, the manifold wisdom of God should be made known to the rulers and authorities in the heavenly realms, according to his eternal purpose which he accomplished in Christ Jesus our Lord (Ephesians 3:10-11).

The question is, "How faithful am I being, as a disciple in the Lord's church, to the call from God to be his spokesperson to a lost world?"

The Danger of Silence

Recently, following a church service, I went over to greet a brand new brother who had just been baptized. He was so excited to be in the kingdom and appreciated the crowd of well-wishers gathered about him. During my conversation with him, he turned toward another brother who was there and said in a light-hearted, yet serious, way, "I've seen and talked to this brother for three years at my job and he never shared with me. He never invited me to church!" You can imagine how guilty that other brother felt hearing this from someone who had just stepped out of the waters of baptism. The reason this other brother hung his head as I looked over at him was because he *was* guilty. Who might be able to say the same thing to you in the fellowship following a Sunday service? Our silence can greatly endanger the souls of other people.

About a year and half ago, during a time when I was looking for a way to get myself out of an evangelistic rut, I asked several Christians where I practiced medicine once a week to join me for a lunchtime Bible study and to invite other coworkers to attend. We assembled this small band of disciples and began having Bible studies at a nearby Chinese restaurant.

For the next several months it was encouraging to see many people come and be genuinely moved by the word of God. Over time, changing schedules prevented us from continuing, but several months later I received the greatest thrill when one of the women who had attended the Bible study approached me at work. I knew that shortly after attending our study she had started studying the Bible in a sector of the church near where she lives. She joyfully informed me that she had confessed Jesus as Lord and had been baptized that past Sunday! Praise God that he helped us and that we were not silent!

Let us realize like never before that God's true church is a place where silence is not an option, and let's speak out like never before. A lost world waits to hear!

LIFE APPLICATION

Who was not silent in your life? What difference has their speaking made in your relationship to God?

On a scale from one to ten (with "one" being "no problem"), how difficult it is for you naturally to speak up and let others know of your convictions? If your answer is between six and ten, what help are you getting from God? From others?

What kind of church would you have if speaking out for Jesus Christ ever became an option—something just for those more naturally inclined to speak?

In what ways is the church you are a part of speaking boldly in our world?

9 Where Love Is Supreme

JEFF CHACON
Tampa, Florida

"A new command I give you: Love one another. As I have loved you, so you must love one another. By this all men will know that you are my disciples, if you love one another."

John 13:34-35

Jesus loved people like no one else. He looked past leprosy to see a beautiful face distorted with pain. And he took the pain away. He looked past gender and race differences and saw lonely hearts crying out for compassion. And he had compassion on them. When Jesus saw people, he didn't see problems. He saw needs. And he saw himself as the one who would meet their needs, as "the good shepherd" who cared enough to teach them right from wrong, to challenge their hearts and even rebuke them when their hearts weren't right. Jesus didn't resent people; he related to them. And then he discipled them. That was the essence of his love.

When the time for Jesus' departure grew near and he gave his disciples the new command to love each other as he had loved them, it was certainly challenging, and it was certainly new. It challenged them to the very core of their being, for they had to know that none of them loved like Jesus did. And it was new in that it was deeper and more unconditional than anything they had ever seen. But in Jesus' mind it was the only way. This is the way it would have to be in his church. His church must practice and be known for this kind of radical love. This was the only way disciples would make it through the trials and the only way that a lost world would be saved.

How are followers of Jesus going to stay in the race to the very end? With the help of others who love like Jesus loved. How are people going to find Jesus today? Through disciples who have said we will love one another in the church as Jesus loved us.

Make It to the End

None of us can make it to the end by ourselves. In our pride we tend to rely on ourselves, even though we let ourselves down over and over again. But the glory of God is seen in the church when we humble ourselves to get the help from God and each other that we need to make it to the end. We cannot do it alone!

> Brothers, if someone is caught in a sin, you who are spiritual should restore him gently....Carry each other's burdens, and in this way you fulfill the law of Christ (Galatians 6:1-2).

Personally, I don't know where I would be without the timely help of other disciples in my life. I'll never forget the "life-giving rebuke" (Proverbs 15:31) that Bruce Williams gave me during a most important time when the church in San Diego was being called back to our original commitment to Jesus and discipleship. He pointed out that my pride manifested itself in a tendency to be critical of other people. In my blindness, I had never seen myself that way before. But once he showed it to me, I began to look back on my life and could see an obvious pattern of criticalness, especially toward those in authority in my life. My criticalness had been a defense mechanism that kept people in authority at arm's length. No wonder I wasn't close to them! No wonder I couldn't trust those in leadership.

That loving challenge in my life was like Jesus removing scales from my eyes. Now some of my best friends in the world are those who have been my leaders. As Jesus' love moved him to restore sight to the blind, so the love of my friend and discipler moved him to challenge the pride and criticalness that was blinding me as well. That's the kind of love that is going to help you and me make it to the end.

Show the World

The world is baffled by the kind of love we find in Jesus. At first people may mistrust what they don't understand. In the world correction is often harsh, and love is sentimental. There is not the combination of "grace and truth" that Jesus brings to our relationships. But to those with open hearts, the love of Christ will have its impact.

Where else can you find blacks and whites hugging, old and young singing, and parents and teenagers enjoying each other's company? The greatest miracle since the resurrection is the miracle of reconciled relationships in the church!

Recently, disciples in our congregation came in contact with a black woman in her mid 60s who had once been a powerful ministry leader in an all-black denomination. Now, she was in the later stages of cancer and in great physical pain. She loved visiting the Orlando church, but her pride had kept her from studying the Bible with anyone. A young white woman working as an intern on our staff attempted to visit and share with her, but she would not allow a white woman into her house.

Finally, with an estimated twenty-four hours to live, the woman's daughter, a true disciple, talked her mom into studying the Bible with the intern. She became convicted of her sins, including her hatred and resentment of white people and admitted that she had known for years that her prejudice was sinful and that it separated her from God. The once-embittered woman was completely broken by the cross and repented on her deathbed. Coming out of the waters of baptism, she immediately sought out the woman who had studied with her and said, "I don't hate you anymore. When I look at you, I don't see white any more." And then, reaching over to take her hand, she said, "I love you."

Only in the church. Only through discipleship. Only the love of Jesus Christ can do that. No one need ever wonder who the people of God are—just look for the people who love each other as Jesus loved.

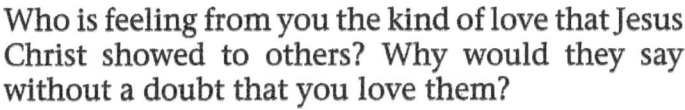

LIFE APPLICATION

Who is feeling from you the kind of love that Jesus Christ showed to others? Why would they say without a doubt that you love them?

Do you see discipling (having someone encourage you, correct you and even rebuke you) as love or as an unwelcome intrusion into your life?

Are you grateful for the "life-giving rebukes" and for those who gave them? Have you told them so?

What do outsiders see in your relationships with other disciples that shows them something unique?

10 Where Fellowship Is Rich

STEVE STATEN
Chicago, Illinois

> They devoted themselves to the apostles' teaching and to the fellowship, to the breaking of bread and to prayer. Everyone was filled with awe, and many wonders and miraculous signs were done by the apostles. All the believers were together and had everything in common. Selling their possessions and goods, they gave to anyone as he had need. Every day they continued to meet together in the temple courts. They broke bread in their homes and ate together with glad and sincere hearts, praising God and enjoying the favor of all the people. And the Lord added to their number daily those who were being saved.
>
> Acts 2:42-47

"This should be illegal! People shouldn't be able to have this much fun." These were the words of a participant in a recent Midwest churches' fellowship weekend where five-thousand gathered together with glad and sincere hearts. Disciples converged on Chicago to enjoy a scheduled weekend of fellowship. What was happening was reminiscent of Acts 2. Every time the true church of God comes together, the fellowship should be rich, even out-of-this-world!

Throughout Old Testament times, Israel assembled for jubilant festivities, feasts, victory celebrations and remembrances. Pentecost, the celebration of the giving of the Law, was to be such an occasion. However, with the convergence upon Jerusalem of the many factions of Jews, "fellowship" is not exactly the best word to describe what would have been going on in 30 A.D. Present on this day would have been Hebraic Jews (including Sadducees, Zealots and Pharisees), Grecian Jews, non-kosher Jews and Ethiopian (black) Jews. True fellowship would have been hindered by competitiveness (much like that which is found in denominations today), radically different priorities and, no doubt, an abundance of arrogance and religious pride. But for at least 3,000 people, something happened that opened the doors to an amazing fellowship.

Three successive building blocks appear in Acts—conviction, apostolic teaching and sacrifice.

Conviction

On the day that the Spirit was poured out in Jerusalem, only one thing could unite the Jews who were split into rigid parties. The verse in Acts 2 that holds the first key to rich fellowship is found in verse 37: "When the people heard this, they were cut to the heart." Those gathered all shared a fresh spiritual wound— they saw their responsibility for the death of Christ. And they all, after seeing their part in Jesus' death, surrendered to God and publicly were baptized in the name of Jesus. This experience was to stay fresh on their minds. As newly freed and forgiven disciples, they were no longer identified by the factions of their past, but by their shared conversion experience. They saw the same God work in different people with the same message and the same result—a new birth. They were brothers and sisters now at the deepest level.

Apostolic Teaching

The second key to rich fellowship was the apostles' teaching. For the first time ever the Holy Spirit, through the apostles, was unleashing the full explanation of the events that had transpired from the Passover through Pentecost. It was the first time they (or anyone) heard about the work of God in Christ at the cross and through the resurrection, the culmination of the expectations of the prophets. Such teaching fills the soul's longing for direction and deep answers. The believers now truly had the same hope, the same purpose in life and the same newfound Lord about whom they were learning. Later the Holy Spirit would be working to inspire the writings of the apostles which would enable future generations to come to faith. Today we can be united by that same teaching.

Sacrifice

The third key to creating deep fellowship was sacrifice. Just a few days earlier, prior to becoming disciples, the Greek pilgrims were expecting to return to the comforts of their homelands: The Hebraic Jews were expecting to return to their homes in Judea and Galilee, and the locals were expecting to have their homes free of guests! None of them were expecting the events of this special Pentecost, and they were all inconvenienced. But who cared? The dreams of the prophets were being fulfilled among them. When one is caught up into such a great drama, sacrifice does not seem so difficult. It seems that they were eager to forfeit their rights of privacy, possessions and privileges to meet each other's needs.

This life-changing event was not the result of an efficiently run conference in the Jerusalem Hyatt. In such a challenging circumstance, selfishness is radically exposed. Thousands of real flesh-and-blood sinners were together taking it one day at a time with no four-color brochure to give them assurance for schedules and meal plans. They had to rely on each other and the inner work of the Holy Spirit to meet the needs. God's plan worked. This all happened before the hard-hearted critics in Jerusalem could gather their first line of attack against the infant church.

Modern-Day "Pentecost"

At the Midwest gathering previously mentioned, the following sentiments were heard which clearly echoed the fellowship of Acts 2:

> "Every age, color and group is represented here. There are no clergy/laity feelings, and we don't have to watch our backs."
> "We shared our food with each other."
> "My face hurt so much from smiling all weekend."
> "I was constantly called upon to do more, and I enjoyed it!"
> "We shared our conversion stories, and everyone wanted to hear them."

As long as the richness of fellowship is viewed in light of the prevailing emptiness of worldly relationships, we will be grateful for what God has done among us—he has convicted us, taught us and helped us sacrifice for each other. It should be no surprise that the result will be the Lord adding many more who are being saved!

LIFE APPLICATION

How have you found that mutual conviction leads to richer fellowship? Would you say that you and those you are with in the church share mutual convictions? How do you know?

Concerning the apostles' teaching (now preserved for us in the Scriptures), how do you find that devotion to these teachings creates a richer fellowship? How does it keep your fellowship from drifting into shallowness?

How would you have felt to be among those described in Acts 2 who "had everything in common" and said that nothing was their own? Is the fellowship in your church as rich as it was in theirs?

What is one thing you would like to change about the fellowship you now experience with other disciples, and what can you do to change it?

11 Where Race Never Matters

JAVIER AMAYA
Boston, Massachusetts

"Nazareth! Can anything good come from there?"
John 1:46

"You are a Jew and I am a Samaritan woman. How can you ask me for a drink?" (For Jews do not associate with Samaritans.)
John 4:9

Just then [Jesus'] disciples returned and were surprised to find him talking with a woman.
John 4:27

"Why does your teacher eat with tax collectors and 'sinners'?"
Matthew 9:11

You are all sons of God through faith in Christ Jesus, for all of you who were baptized into Christ have clothed yourselves with Christ.
Galatians 3:26-27

Actions, statements and behaviors only explained by the evils of prejudice, racism, classism and ignorance have always been a part of the human experience. Our tendency is to look for what separates us, not what unites us. However, in the church of God we are all a new creation! Whether white or black, Latino or Asian, there is a vital role for each of us in *his* church. In recent years we have seen God's movement "move" from its mostly white, American, middle-class origin into a multiracial, multicultural, multilingual worldwide fellowship. In the world, race matters a lot. In the kingdom of God it matters *not at all.*

As we exit the waters of baptism, all the distinctions come to an end. However, prejudice, like any other sin, must be renounced in an ongoing way. God is glorified when we totally eradicate sin at its root, not simply its outward appearance.

Consider your own life, not just whether your church is multiracial or socially heterogeneous.

- Is at least one of your five closest friends of a different race and/or social background?
- Who do your kids play with?
- How do you react to an interracial couple?
- Do you deny your roots or utilize them to expand the kingdom?
- Do you share your faith with every type of person?
- Is there anyone you would hesitate to have in your home because of their racial or social status?
- Ask someone from a different background if they have observed any prejudices in you.

An End to Elitism

Growing up, I was exposed to many cultures due to my parents' business. By the eighth grade I had lived in five different countries and had gone to eight different schools. Going into Brown University, I prided myself on being a well-rounded and open person. However, as I look back I see what a sheltered, prejudiced and classist attitude I had. I made it a point to speak both English and Spanish without an accent. I was careful to wear the right clothes and brag about the area of town we lived in and even my education. I was an elitist snob. I remember being ashamed of being seen with our maid in the street, for fear that she would be mistaken for my sister. The elitism was so blatant that my freshman year of college my friends and I believed that only a few of us in the world were "true thinkers" and that the rest simply survived life without truly thinking. We divided the world into the "thinking few" (Ivy Leaguers) and "the rest."

I praise God for his kingdom because it broke down so many walls of prejudice that kept me from knowing others and valuing their lives. I am part of an interracial marriage; though, honestly, I have never thought of it as such. Kelly is white American and I am Latino. Our closest relationships during the last twelve years as disciples have varied widely in class and race, and we are so much the better for it.

It has been such a joy to be involved with people for whom educational, racial or professional credentials are insignificant. I remember in Boston having tremendous relationships with many who didn't know what an Ivy League school was. In Miami we developed relationships that will last through eternity with blacks, whites, Latinos, Jamaicans and many others. In Mexico, our closest relationships vary from housekeepers to well-to-do businessmen.

We have been able to take Diana and Elena, our two daughters, to meet and play with all kinds of children, from the children at the HOPE Worldwide projects in Mexico's "casas de carton" (cardboard houses), to the exclusive neighborhoods of Palm Beach. They are learning to value all children alike.

Kelly is a woman of great sensitivity and flexibility. She has made it a point to learn, respect and value the differences in other cultures. Whether it is food, clothing, music or social idiosyncrasies, she has always looked to see what is special and worthy of praising, imitating and incorporating into our lives. Now she is almost mistaken for a Latino herself!

I praise God for being part of a church that is making history in combating racial prejudice. Our challenge as we find new frontiers kingdomwide is to be able to break loose from the sin of prejudice in each of our hearts. Philippians 2:3 challenges disciples to "in humility consider others better than yourselves." Our way of living, acting, thinking, eating, dressing or our color is no better—it is just different than others'.

How sad and sinful it would be to close ourselves into a limited world and let the precious jewels of the experiences, cultures, personalities and strengths of so many pass us by. What would life be without American football, the World Cup, the Ryder Cup, Jamaican jerk chicken, Puerto Rican rice and beans, real Mexican tacos, Colombian coffee, New England clam chowder, sushi, mariachi, rock and roll, Cumbias, Haitian limbo dancing, jazz, white friends, black friends, poor friends, rich friends and so on...? Praise God that in his church, we don't have to know.

LIFE APPLICATION

It has been said that eleven o'clock on Sunday morning is the most segregated hour in America. You may not live in America, but what does this say about "the church" that could be described like this? What does it mean if a church preaches acceptance of all races, but has no ethnic and racial diversity?

What did your own upbringing teach you about race and class differences?

Who was your first close friend who was very different ethnically or racially from you?

As a disciple, in what ways have you changed your thoughts and attitudes towards those different from yourself?

12 Where Family Is Restored

JIMMY ROGERS
Boston, Massachusetts

> But now in Christ Jesus you who once were far away have been brought near through the blood of Christ.
> For he himself is our peace, who has made the two one and has destroyed the barrier, the dividing wall of hostility, by abolishing in his flesh the law with its commandments and regulations. His purpose was to create in himself one new man out of the two, thus making peace, and in this one body to reconcile both of them to God through the cross, by which he put to death their hostility. He came and preached peace to you who were far away and peace to those who were near. For through him we both have access to the Father by one Spirit.
> Ephesians 2:13-18

The best qualities of strong families should show up everywhere in the church of Jesus Christ. I grew up in a household where my mom and dad stressed that nothing was more important than family. We *loved* to be together. Coming from an Italian family, mealtimes were almost a worship experience when we would sit for hours and just enjoy each other's company. I have three brothers and a sister, and we always loved being together, whether working or playing. I also remember, as siblings, we would occasionally fight with each other, but we always worked through our differences with tears and love. We were very protective when it came to attacks by those outside the family. I could never understand how families could disown one of their members or how they could talk badly about each other to people.

My family was not perfect, but my experiences gave me some very good ideas about what God wanted when he called his church a family.

A Father's Love

At the heart of a family must be a parent. As the theme passage teaches us, we start out "far away" from God and his love, but through the blood of Jesus, his one and only Son, we can become his children. We were all orphans, lonely and lost, crying out to be loved and wanted. There is no more vivid description of heartfelt pain than that of a child with no mommy or daddy to hold and love him as their own. This is God's view of us when we are without a relationship with him. He longs to reconcile us to himself through the cross. God so wanted a relationship with each of us individually that he was willing to destroy the barrier of sin that kept us far from him—even though it cost him his own Son's life. "How great is the love the father has lavished on us, that we should be called children of God! And that is what we are!" (1 John 3:1).

As God's children we can communicate with him freely, with confidence and peace because we know that we belong to him. "God sent the Spirit of his Son into our hearts, the Spirit who calls out '*Abba*, Father'" (Galatians 4:6). "Abba"—"Daddy." No one before Jesus had ever dared to be as intimate with God as he was. He showed us how to be emotionally close to our heavenly Father. Nothing can ever tear us away from that relationship—but we *can* leave of our own volition. Someone once said, "If you're not close to God, guess who moved?" God's love is immovable and immeasurable.

God's Adopted Family

In addition to the relationship we can have with God personally, we can also share this relationship with each other. No matter what our differences, whether age, race, education, social status, wealth or looks, we are now one family perfectly united in Christ as his body, the church. Only the power and love of God could destroy the barriers that the world has created between men and women of all nations.

Our love for God is manifested specifically through our love for one another. God desires to see his children love each other, encourage one another and be there for each other in good times and in difficult times. The family of God, living in harmony and love, is the greatest testimony that we are truly Jesus' disciples. Our relationships are a vital key to God's plan for winning the world back to himself. People must see that, though we aren't perfect, nothing will destroy or separate us from our love and commitment to God, our Father, and to each other.

What stops the church from being the family God wants us to be? *Sin*: independence, selfishness, pride, insecurity and fear. These get in the way of the deep, loving relationships God wants us to have with one another. But we absolutely must not give in to these things and lose the gift of family God is giving us. We must not forget the love God has given us—love we now possess to give to others.

A Flesh-and-Blood Example

I am privileged to oversee a ministry in Boston's inner city where I have seen God's plan for family come alive. There, 75% of children are born out of wedlock—the highest per capita rate in the U.S. Many of the disciples did not grow up with a father. One brother grew up in a single-mom family of twelve and has never seen his father. He saw many of his brothers and sisters given up for adoption; he saw his brothers beat his mother beyond recognition. He learned to get his security and relationships from drugs and alcohol and the people who used them. This was his definition of "family."

After becoming a disciple, he learned how to support his brothers and sisters, to love and sacrifice for them even when it hurt. He learned to forgive his brothers but also learned the value of being forgiven. He realized his sin beat Jesus beyond recognition and yet Jesus, his brother, has completely forgiven him. Most of all he learned security through having a Father who will never leave him and having brothers and sisters who truly love and believe in him no matter what.

LIFE APPLICATION

When God designed family, what do you think he had in mind?

In what ways have you seen God's plan for family fulfilled in the church?

Do imperfections in the family keep you from enjoying all the many positive aspects of life among God's people?

What can you do this week to strengthen the bonds of family among the disciples with whom you live and work?

How do you handle it when you have a conflict in God's family?

13 Where Gifts Differ

Scotland

> Just as each of us has one body with many members, and these members do not all have the same function, so in Christ we who are many form one body, and each member belongs to all the others.
>
> Romans 12:4-5

The beauty of the church is its simplicity—its unity in diversity. We are *not* all the same; we are widely (sometimes wildly) different. The true church of Christ is a dynamic interplay of different gifts and abilities; it's the place "where gifts differ." If we ignore this fact, we hurt not only ourselves, but also God's plans for his church. A square peg does not fit happily into a round hole.

Unity in Diversity

God has given each of us different gifts and talents. Some gifts we have had for a long time; others we pick up as we go. What are your gifts? For me, cooking is definitely not one of my gifts. If I have to, I cook. Otherwise, I let my wife have the honors. Although I quite enjoy sports, I am not a particularly fast runner. Fortunately, my survival does not usually depend on my cooking and running ability. I prefer to do what I am good at, and this principle applies across the board in the church.

God can also take raw potential and turn it into something useful for the purposes of his kingdom. Take me, for instance. By nature I am an introvert. Expressiveness is not my strong suit. I remember well my first speech in high school: I got an "F." After my first attempt at leading a Bible study, one of my guests patted me on the back and could only say, "Nice try." But God can change us! He has helped me to overcome my inward focus and to become an evangelist and teacher who has spoken to churches in dozens of cities worldwide—and who seldom gets anxious in the face of public speaking. God can develop your latent gifts, too. In fact if he doesn't, you will be unfulfilled.

Gifts in the Bible

There are many gifts mentioned in the Bible. Fewer than half are miraculous abilities given in the apostolic age; most are present today. There are five lists of gifts in the New Testament. Romans 12:6-8 deals with gifts present in the church today. 1 Corinthians 12:8-10 mentions miraculous gifts, while 1 Corinthians 12:28 mixes miraculous with non-miraculous. Ephesians 4:11 indicates leadership positions. Finally, 1 Peter 4:10-11 divides the gifts into two broad categories: speaking and serving. The Old Testament mentions gifts such as artistic and musical ability (Exodus 31:1-11; Psalm 68:25). As disciples we are not all the same, and it's not even desirable that we all be the same. Roles differ, and we must respect and help develop the different gifts our brothers and sisters have.

Case Study: London 1995

The London church, where I serve, is loaded with talented people, but not all had been using their gifts before this year. As a result, church growth had stagnated. This year, the church is growing daily in spirit and numbers because the leadership recognizes we are all different and need each other's strengths (opportunities to help and inspire) and weaknesses (opportunities to serve and be compassionate). Consider Romans 12:6-8:

> We have different gifts, according to the grace given us. If a man's gift is prophesying, let him use it in proportion to his faith. If it is serving, let him serve; if it is teaching, let him teach; if it is encouraging, let him encourage; if it is contributing to the needs of others, let him give generously; if it is leadership, let him govern diligently; if it is showing mercy, let him do it cheerfully.

Prophesying: Bold and visionary messages are preached by the London evangelists. Many men and women see the growth of the church and are considering the ministry as a full-time career.

Serving: Church administrators work hand in hand with ministry staff; children's ministry workers serve our families excellently, and serving responsibilities are clearly delegated so that each project is brought to completion in an inspirational manner.

Teaching: A weekly coordinated teaching program on a churchwide level keeps disciples rooted in the Word. This year the whole church has studied twelve books of the Bible together and five books published by Discipleship Publications International. Teachers are raising up teachers, just as evangelists raise up evangelists.

Encouraging: Our new elders make sure the church is encouraged and on track, while talented song leaders teach us new hymns and keep our spirits high. Specialized ministries are encouraged.

Contributing: Each member gives sacrificially, both to the local church and to world missions—and the giving far exceeds expectations.

Leadership: Leaders lead by personal example. All staff members regularly bring visitors to church and bear fruit. The "mission group leaders" have clear objectives: helping their members to study with at least one non-Christian per week and have friends at church on Sunday. Many new evangelists and women's ministry leaders are being appointed.

Mercy: Our work for the homeless is second to none, and all church members are involved in the work of HOPE Worldwide, helping the poor around the world.

The London church is truly a place "where gifts differ." Through utilizing each member's gifts, God is bringing about a great victory in this city. But the great news is that his plan works in every city.

Some Gift Guidelines

Never place God's commands in the category of "gifts." For instance, some people may have more of a knack for evangelism than others, but everyone is to be evangelistic. Don't make false comparisons between yourself and others (Romans 12:3, Galatians 6:4). What you can do, do well. Trust God—the Spirit will enhance your gifts.

LIFE APPLICATION

Look around you, and see how your brothers and sisters are utilizing their gifts. Encourage them! The church will never be what God means it to be unless we develop the attitude and programs to make the most of each disciple's strengths.

Identify and list your gifts. Be realistic, but faithful. Whatever your gifts, do not boast. Whatever strengths you have come from God (James 1:17).

How thankful are you for your gifts? How blessed do you feel that you have gifts to use for God?

How can you use your gifts to help others (1 Peter 4:10)? Tell your leaders how you want to help. What spiritual blessings will we receive when we are focused on giving to others?

14 Where Unity Is a Passion

Nick Young

> As a prisoner of the Lord, then, I urge you to live a life worthy of the calling you have received. Be completely humble and gentle; be patient, bearing with one another in love. Make every effort to keep the unity of the Spirit through the bond of peace. There is one body and one Spirit—just as you were called to one hope when you were called—one Lord, one faith, one baptism; one God and Father of all, who is over all and through all and in all.
>
> Ephesians 4:1-6

One of the characteristics of the heart of Paul was his passion for unity within the body of Christ. Paul believed that unity among the believers was an identifying mark of a healthy church. He believed that disunity indicated spiritual disease. In 1 Corinthians 1:10, he appealed to the church, in the name of our Lord Jesus Christ, that they all "agree with one another so that there may be no divisions among you and that you may be perfectly united in mind and thought." He sought a perfect unity. Just as the human body must operate in unity, the body of Christ, also, must have unity. We need to be of the same mind and have the same purpose and the same focus. In Philippians 1:27, Paul says that we need to "stand firm in one Spirit, contending *as one man* for the faith of the gospel" (emphasis added). What a marvelous picture of unity!

Fight for It

How must our passion for unity be demonstrated? First, we need to *fight* for it. We are by nature sinful, prideful, deceitful and contentious. In the best of us, this is true. Unity is not "just going to happen." Unity will happen because we fight for it. This is true in the family, in marriage, on the athletic field and, most of all, in the kingdom of God. Remember, Paul says we need to make every effort to maintain unity.

Challenge Sin

Second, we must challenge sin. Sin divides people. Galatians 2:11-14 says,

> When Peter came to Antioch, I opposed him to his face because, he was clearly in the wrong. Before certain men came from James, he used to eat with the Gentiles. But when they arrived, he began to draw back and separate himself from the Gentiles because he was afraid of those who belonged to the circumcision group. The other Jews joined him in his hypocrisy, so that by their hypocrisy even Barnabas was led astray.
>
> When I saw that they were not acting in line with the truth of the gospel, I said to Peter in front of them all, "You are a Jew, yet you live like a Gentile and not like a Jew. How is it, then, that you force Gentiles to follow Jewish customs?"

The hypocrisy in Peter's life separated him and those who followed him from the others who were pure. Sin divides us still. When it appears, it must be addressed in order for unity to be restored. It is not fun to challenge or to be challenged; yet sometimes it must be done to bring unity. The matter may not need to be dealt with in a public setting, at least not at first (see the discussion of Matthew 18:15-17 below), but sin must never be swept under the rug. It also should be noted that no one in the church is above challenge. A leader in sin needs to be corrected just as any other member.

Resolve Conflict

Third, we must resolve conflict quickly. Though we are the Lord's church, we still may have some occasional conflict arise in our everyday relationships. Married couples learn that love is not a guarantee against conflict. The best of marriages will have some unpleasant times, but these people stay together because they have learned to resolve their problems. So, we must decide in advance that when trouble comes, we will resolve it quickly. Here's what should happen if you have conflict: "Do not let the sun go down while you are still angry, and do not give the devil a foothold" (Ephesians 4:26-27). What happens if you are the offended party, or if you are the offending party? Jesus gives us the clear answers in his remarks recorded in Matthew's account of the gospel. Jesus said,

"If your brother sins against you, go and show him his fault, just between the two of you. If he listens to you, you have won your brother over. But if he will not listen, take one or two others along, so that 'every matter may be established by the testimony of two or three witnesses'" (Matthew 18:15-16).

Additionally, in the Sermon on the Mount, Jesus proclaimed,

"...if you are offering your gift at the altar and there remember that your brother has something against you, leave your gift there in front of the altar. First go and be reconciled to your brother; then come and offer your gift" (Matthew 5:23-24).

Thus, Jesus is teaching that whether you are the person committing the offense or are the one sinned against, you have an equal obligation to reconcile with your brother. Ideally, both parties will meet approximately halfway, when both are humbly seeking reconciliation. In this way unity can be reclaimed. Truly, God's plan is amazing!

Love One Another

Finally, unity is possible when we love each other. Love covers a multitude of sins. In twenty-one years of marriage, Debbie and I have become very much alike in many different areas. Yet, there are still some definite differences between us. But, this is okay. She does not have to be just like me, nor do I have to be just like her in order for us to have unity in our family. Some people erroneously think that to have unity everybody must be just like them. This denies the principle and power of love. Love unifies!

Every disciple should have a passion for unity. Without it, world evangelism will remain only a farfetched dream. With unity in our relationships, though, tough times become fewer and more tolerable, and good times become more numerous and sensational. If we, as God's people, stay united and increase even more in this virtue, then our greatest victories are yet to come!

LIFE APPLICATION

Have you ever been a part of a disunited church or religious body? What contributed to the disunity? What were the effects of the disunity?

What tendencies do you see in yourself that contribute to disunity in the body of Christ?

What specific things can you be doing, even this week, to build unity in the family of God?

Read John 17 and hear Jesus' passion for unity. Pray about your own commitment to the unity of the church.

15 Where the Strong Love the Weak

MARK OTTENWELLER, M.D.
Atlanta, Georgia

> We who are strong ought to bear with the failings of the weak and not to please ourselves.
>
> Romans 15:1

The church is an incredible place. It is the only place on earth where people come in as patients and go out as doctors. When a church is really Jesus' church, it welcomes the weak, loves the weak and strengthens the weak. Because of the tremendous support and challenge in the church, the weak become stronger and stronger, and every disciple grows to become more and more like Jesus. This is how it works:

God Chooses the Weak

Paul tells us in 1 Corinthians 1:27 that "God chose the weak things of the world to shame the strong." All of us, at one point, were weak. God chose us in spite of our failures and struggles and weaknesses. Sin had destroyed almost all of our character and conviction, but God rescued us from ourselves and from all of our sins. Then with much effort, he made us strong. God chooses the weak because they know they need help. They respond to him and are thankful; as a result, they bring glory to him.

I have always had a weak character. During my college days I was well-known for "crayfishing" (rapidly retreating in the face of conflict). In spite of my cowardice, God discipled me and raised me up to lead the HOPE Worldwide projects in Africa. I was once afraid to move to New York, so God took me to war-torn Rwanda, malaria-ridden Nigeria, and riot- and AIDS-plagued South Africa. God took a weak man, worked on his character and put him in many situations were he could reach out to other weak and needy men.

Help the Weak

"In everything I did, I showed you that by this kind of hard work we must help the weak," said Paul in Acts 20:35. It is never easy to help the weak. It is always too early or too late or too inconvenient. It always takes more time and seems more tiring than anything else we do, but it is one of the most important things we can do. God uses the weak to build and mold our character and our heart. The hard work changes us and teaches us to love anyone from any place with any problem. Then we truly become like Jesus.

The weak teach us more than we could ever teach them. We desperately need them as much as they need us. The church and its leaders will only grow in their hearts as they grow in their outreach to the weak. To help the weak, each disciple must feel with people as Jesus did. He was filled with compassion (or filled with other people's feelings). He must have often asked himself, "How do they feel?" and "Why do they feel that way?" We, as disciples, must ask ourselves the same questions.

Several years ago when our daughter Leslie had cerebral malaria and began to hallucinate, I was afraid that she might die. Those fears did not end until she was strong and back to health. No family can sit back and relax when there is a sick child among them. So it is in the church. No one can relax until everyone is strong. Just as we feed and nourish our children every day to keep them strong, so we must not neglect to feed and nourish the weak in the church. Every disciple must be fed every day in order to be strong and to grow. There is no acceptable reason for disciples to be neglected and to become weak. We need to love the weak the way we love our own children; if we do, they will become strong.

The Weak Shame the Strong

God's power to change the weak into the strong is incredible. As we allow God to change us, others are inspired by our growth. As we overcome struggles, face challenges and become stronger, we inspire others to have greater faith. The greater the challenge, the greater the inspiration. As our weaknesses become our strengths, everyone in the church becomes stronger, especially the weak.

It is amazing how much impact people who have been weak can have on the "strong" of this world. People do not expect to see weaknesses become strengths, and when it happens people are amazed. It grabs their attention because most people long to change. Jesus was crucified in weakness, yet by God's power, he was raised in strength (1 Corinthians 15:42; 2 Corinthians 13:4). He came from weakness and had impact on the strong. Thank God we can, with his power, do the same.

A great example of weakness becoming strength is the life of Blaise Okale. As a young disciple in Abidjan, he really struggled. He got involved in sin and wanted to give up, to return to the world. His temptations had become seemingly too difficult to overcome, and spiritual success seemed impossible. But we encouraged him, and he did not give up. Through the grace of God he became stronger and stronger. After becoming the first French-speaking evangelist in the church, he planted the church in Douala, Cameroon, where he now lives with his wife and two children, inspiring French-speaking disciples all over Africa. He who was once weak now shames the strong.

God Increases the Power of the Weak

> Do you not know?
>   Have you not heard?
> The LORD is the everlasting God,
>   the Creator of the ends of the earth.
> He will not grow tired or weary,
>   and his understanding no one can fathom.
> He gives strength to the weary
>   and increases the power of the weak.
> Even youths grow tired and weary,
>   and young men stumble and fall;
> but those who hope in the LORD
>   will renew their strength.
> They will soar on wings like eagles;
>   they will run and not grow weary,
>   they will walk and not be faint.
>   Isaiah 40:28-31

In his church, God never gives up on us when we are weak. Let us praise him that he strengthens us and enables us to strengthen others.

Editors' note: Dr. Mark Ottenweller was named Person of the Week in December 1995 by ABC News for his compassionate work with HIV-positive and AIDS patients in South Africa.

LIFE APPLICATION

In comparison to God, are you weak or are you strong? How does your answer affect the way you look at others?

Are you harsh or self-righteous toward the weak? Are you too busy? Too quick to refer the weak to others or to write them off?

Do the weak become disciples *because of* you or *in spite of* you? Why?

Which weak disciples have you helped to become strong?

Who in your life right now needs love and patience from you in order to become strong? Who has been patient with you to help you to grow?

16 Where Leaders Are Servants

MARK TEMPLER

> To the elders among you, I appeal as a fellow elder, a witness of Christ's sufferings and one who also will share in the glory to be revealed: Be shepherds of God's flock that is under your care, serving as overseers—not because you must, but because you are willing, as God wants you to be; not greedy for money, but eager to serve; not lording it over those entrusted to you, but being examples to the flock. And when the Chief Shepherd appears, you will receive the crown of glory that will never fade away.
>
> 1 Peter 5:1-4

It was the spring of 1984. I was in my final year of my master's program in political science at the Massachusetts Institute of Technology (MIT), and I had just made the decision to become a disciple. One night, on the eve of an exam, I was asked by another disciple if I could help a young freshman who was struggling with physics and preparing for an exam of his own the next day. My friend knew that my undergraduate degree was in physics, but he did not know that during all my years at MIT, I had never helped anyone prepare for an exam. At times, I had exchanged help with others, but I had never served anyone if it did not benefit me.

That evening, instead of studying for my own exam, I went across campus to this young man's dormitory. I spent three hours helping him to prepare. He made great progress during this time. I don't know how he did on his exam—he never told me. I don't remember how I did on my exam, but I do remember walking back from his dorm in the cold night air, looking at the stars and weeping. I had never felt that way before. I felt a joy, a glory, a sense of righteousness that I had never known. I had finally experienced the feeling that results from serving others unconditionally.

Examples, Not Bosses

The world is full of bosses and administrators who are "impressive" people. But, God is looking for *servants* to lead the people in his church. In this passage, Peter was writing specifically to elders, but the principles are applicable to all Christians. He "appealed" (from the Greek *parakaolo*) to them as a peer, a fellow elder, someone who had seen Jesus. Peter did not want to lord it over them, but rather, to appeal to the goodness within their own hearts so that they would do what was right. Peter knew that people respond better when their leaders believe in them—when they are "appealed to" for help rather than commanded coldly to obey.

In 1 Peter 5:2, Peter called on the elders to be shepherds, taking care of the flock. He wanted them to *serve*. (This was the same charge that Jesus had given Peter himself in John 21:15-17.) Peter wanted the elders to be motivated not by obligation or greed, but by eagerness to give. His method of leadership was simple: They were to serve as examples, not act as bosses (1 Peter 5:3). Glory in God's kingdom comes not through position, but through suffering servanthood (1 Peter 5:4). This is what Jesus lived; this is how we must live.

Light the Fire

Peter understood an important principle. When a leader lords it over his followers, he builds into them a desire to rebel. When he is an oppressive leader, his followers build walls to protect themselves. Loyalty disappears and openness is replaced by "saying the right thing" so as not to get into trouble. But when a leader cares for people and appeals to their hearts, drawing out their good, he ignites in them a fire of loyalty and zeal. This is the fire Jesus lit in Legion when he drove out the demons and sent him home to preach in Mark 5. This is the fire Jesus lit in Peter when he cooked him breakfast, forgave his denial and called him to be a shepherd in John 21. This is the fire Jesus lit in Paul when he humbled him, healed him and told him to preach to all men in Acts 9.

In God's church today, we light a fire when we demonstrate a zeal and joy for serving others unconditionally. When our leadership is characterized by example and servanthood, it produces a passion that moves hearts when we preach and teach.

Raj Mohan Paul and his wife, Rani, are disciples whose hearts are on fire for Jesus. Baptized in Bangalore, India, in 1988, they gave up promising careers in the world to become ministry interns. As young leaders, they learned to serve others: taking care of children, running errands, helping the poor and sick and encouraging the weak. In December 1991, they were called to lead the Madras church, a struggling group in need of love. But even in becoming leaders of a church, they have kept their servant hearts, doing the little things that make a difference. They constantly entertain others in their home—at least forty people pass through their house every day. They have invited relatives to come live with them. Because of their example, a dozen of their relatives have been baptized into Christ!

During one period, Raj Mohan Paul had not borne fruit in ten months, so he went on a five-day fast. Soon afterward, he met a family of five people who were all baptized into Christ, and one is now an intern! Besides taking care of their own son, Steven, two years ago the Pauls adopted a baby named Shalini, a little girl with a severe cleft palate. The impact of their constant service has been amazing: Hundreds of hearts have been set on fire for Christ. In four years their one church of about one-hundred members has multiplied into four congregations with 700 disciples, 500 of whom are in Madras!

In God's church we must never become like the world, where leaders will often think they should be served rather than serve. Movements become monuments when leaders cease to serve and become focused more on personal comfort. We must remember that perspiration and inspiration lead to multiplication, but indulgent relaxation and selfish delegation lead to stagnation. Let us once again feel the joy and the glory that comes from being sold-out servants in God's kingdom!

LIFE APPLICATION

All of us have felt the joy of servanthood. Do you remember the first time you felt the joy of serving unconditionally as a disciple? Have you felt that joy lately?

Peter said that elders should not be greedy for money, but eager to serve. What do you think about most of the time? Are you thinking a lot about your possessions, your finances, your home-improvement projects? Or God and other souls?

Has your Christian life stagnated into a schedule of rituals, satisfying accountability rather than caring for others? Do you lead by serving and caring for others or by quickly delegating? How can you change in these areas?

How can you, as a leader or a follower, inspire others to be on fire for Jesus?

17 Where Followers Bring Joy

> Remember your leaders, who spoke the word of God to you. Consider the outcome of their way of life and imitate their faith.
>
> Hebrews 13:7

> Obey your leaders and submit to their authority. They keep watch over you as men who must give an account. Obey them so that their work will be a joy, not a burden, for that would be of no advantage to you.
>
> Hebrews 13:17

Our human nature does not intrinsically long to imitate or to submit. In fact, our more typical response is to be suspicious, critical and prideful towards those who have authority over us in any way. I saw evidence of my own stubborn nature early in life. Once I was confronted by my high school principal for violating the school policy of not sitting on the hall floors. He told me to stand up. I, however, remained seated for a long time before rising reluctantly and defiantly to stand before a very flustered and angry man. On another occasion when I was in an assembly, I remained seated when my name was called to come up on stage to receive an honors award. Then I had the nerve to appear in the principal's office later that same day and demand my honors pin. I was a long way from grasping and obeying God's will for me to have a submissive spirit toward those in authority over me.

Leadership Is God's Plan

In Ephesians 3, Paul calls the people to bring God "glory in the church." The remaining chapters of the letter tell us how to do that. Paul makes it clear that God has called some to be leaders and the rest to be followers. The purpose behind this plan is that we might be equipped "for works of service" (Ephesians 4:12), that we will "grow up into...Christ" (4:15) and that the body might grow as it "builds itself up in love, as each part does its work" (4:16). In this context, it is the work of the leaders to lead and the work of the followers to follow. When, and only when, this takes place, will growth occur and God be glorified in his church.

Nonspiritual people look at this plan and its effect on our lives as disciples and wonder how we can be so naive. Are we brainwashed? Have we taken leave of our senses? We've done neither! We absolutely trust that the God who gave some to be "apostles and prophets" and whose authority we absolutely accept for our lives, is the same God who gave some to be "evangelists, pastors and teachers." We are confident about those who lead us because we are convinced that God has chosen them. God's choosing is confirmed to us as we "consider the outcome of their way of life" and therefore, we have no problem understanding that we should both imitate and submit to the leaders God has put in our lives. As long as we realize that submission to man should never override our submission to God, we can maintain a healthy, biblical perspective.

Submission Is God's Demand

In Romans 13:1-2, Paul challenges all disciples to "submit...to the governing authorities, for there is no authority except that which God has established." And just in case that went over our heads he says again, "The authorities that exist have been established by God." Therefore, to show disrespect and to be disobedient to these "secular" authorities is to rebel against God. Brothers and sisters, if that is how we must view and respond to the governing authorities in our world, how much more the authorities God has instituted to lead and govern his church? There is no excuse whatsoever for disrespect and disobedience. Rebellion, in all its forms, is an act of the sinful nature and must be crucified (Galatians 5:16-25). When it is, glory is brought to God in his church.

Before becoming a disciple of Jesus, I was a minister of a denominational church in which I seldom saw an attitude of submission from those who were being led. In turn, I saw many leaders whose vision and determination were crushed by the cynicism, criticism and suspicion they constantly had to face in the membership. What a joy and what a challenge it was for me to be introduced to a church with people who, because of their submission to God, loved, supported, encouraged, obeyed, imitated and respected the leaders God had given them. Disciples were growing so quickly! So many people were being won to Christ! My family and I packed our possessions and moved to be part of this church, God's kingdom on this earth.

Now that I am one of those "some" whom God has "given" to lead his church, "I myself am a man under authority..." and so are those who lead me (Luke 7:8). One of the things that gives disciples even more confidence in their leaders is to see that they show the same respect for those who lead them. I have seen no better example of this than the lead evangelist of our congregation, Tony Singh. Recently a decision was reached that did not seem to have the most favorable short-term consequences for our work. Leaders who were over our family of churches had decided that a man who was being trained by Tony was needed in another congregation. On hearing about the decision, I called Tony, concerned about how he might be feeling since he had devoted so much of his time, energy and heart to the person. How foolish of me! Knowing that God's leaders were involved in making the decision, he felt nothing but the utmost confidence that God's will had been done. Because of his faith in God, he respected the lives and the decisions of the leaders whose lives he was imitating.

As followers of Jesus, may we follow God's plan by having a submissive heart toward the leaders he has chosen. May we each determine to make the work of God's leaders a joy!

LIFE APPLICATION

Do you "remember your leaders who spoke the word of God to you"? As you do, are you grateful for their initial and ongoing efforts to instruct and train you? Write down their names, and spend time today expressing your gratitude to God, to others and to them.

When a leader challenges you individually or collectively to some specific course of action, what is your response? Do you immediately consider how you are going to obey that direction, or do you find a way to excuse yourself? What was the last specific direction given to you by a church leader? Have you done what was asked?

Do you trust God to do a better job than you to hold your leaders accountable for their actions, or do you see yourself as one of the kingdom's watchdogs—always ready to call attention to it when you think a leader has messed up?

Do you "consider the outcome of their way of life," or do you critique their every move? Are you focused on the attributes in their lives that you are imitating, or does the list of qualities that come to mind consist of their weaknesses, miscues, mistakes and sins? Write a very specific list of qualities you see in your leaders that you want to imitate.

PART III

Directed
to
Love

*Apart from loving God, there is
no greater commandment than for us
to love one another. Many New Testament
passages describe our "one another"
relationships and show the church how to
demonstrate life-changing love.*

18 Loving One Another Deeply

KEVIN MCDANIEL

Now that you have purified yourselves by obeying the truth so that you have sincere love for your brothers, love one another deeply, from the heart.

1 Peter 1:22

I had finally arrived at the world's greatest learning institution—the University of Georgia! I was 19 years old and looking forward to experiencing freedom away from my home in Atlanta. Life was truly going to be a party. I checked into Russell Hall, one of the freshman skyscraper dorms, more commonly known as the "Zoo." I liked room 501 where I would soon rest each night in preparation for the next day's celebration.

Shortly after arriving at UGA, I pledged and was initiated into a fraternity. My plans were coming together quickly. Life was going to be what I had always dreamed about: beer, girls and sleep. Then, he entered my life...

John Reus, the resident assistant on my hall, introduced himself to me and during the following six months became unquestionably the best friend I had ever had. What was unusual about this guy was that his Christian beliefs really affected his behavior. I had known many people in the South who called themselves Christians, but I had known very few who had really let God have his way with them. John was a true disciple, the real McCoy. During the first few months of our friendship, as I partied hard and pickled my brains, I saw that he was living the life that I really wanted. I desired happiness and inner peace and sought them through my social life. The drinking and carousing I did were part of a quest to find something pleasurable in a life that was, otherwise, neither fulfilling nor happy.

On the other hand, John and his band of seemingly carefree friends were always happy. In fact, if I was having a bad day, I could spend time with John, Ron, Ward and the other guys, and life seemed better. I couldn't explain it at the time, but there was a sense of peace wherever they went. I liked it. I later realized that what they had was a genuine love for God and each other. Not too long after this, I decided I wanted to be a real Christian just like they were.

The Power of Caring

What compelled me to follow God? It was not doctrinal correctness. It was not because John taught the truth. It was simply because I saw what it meant to be a true disciple: John loved me deeply from the heart. He cared about how I was doing in school, how things were going with my folks and certainly how things were going in my relationship with God. Bottom line: he cared. Other than my family, no one had ever been so genuinely concerned for my well-being.

Then, something really strange began to happen inside of me. I found myself caring for John, my fraternity brothers, the guys on my hall and people in general. "Could this be love?" "Is this genuine selfless concern?" It felt so good not to be absorbed in my own affairs that it frightened me. There would be days when I would catch myself feeling good about life for no apparent reason. A fraternity brother would ask, "Hey, what are you so happy about? Did you ace a test? Find a girl?" No, I was discovering what it meant to be loved and to love...and it was awesome!

Why did John and his buddies from church seem so different to me? It was because they *were* different. Jesus said in John 13:35, "By this all men will know that you are my disciples, if you love one another." Listen to what the Bible teaches about relationships between disciples: "love one another," "be devoted to one another," "honor one another," "live in harmony with one another," "accept one another," "agree with one another," "serve one another," "be patient with one another," "be kind and compassionate to one another," "submit to one another," "teach and admonish one another," "encourage one another daily," "offer hospitality to one another," "clothe yourselves with humility toward one another," and on and on it goes—all the things you are reading and studying about in this book.

Love Helps the Medicine Go Down

Husbands and wives: Are you having some problems? "Submit to one another out of reverence for Christ" (Ephesians 5:21).

Singles: Having some struggles with the roommates? "Bear with each other and forgive whatever grievances you may have against one another. Forgive as the Lord forgave you" (Colossians 3:13).

Students: Are the studies getting you down? "Encourage one another and build each other up" (1 Thessalonians 5:11).

Do you get it? We come to God because of his deep love for us, and we stay with God because of his deep love for us— especially as we see it in one another.

Recently I was talking with a leader about a sister who seemed to be a problem for everyone who tried to work with her. When people came to get advice about how to help her, they always started with all the negative things about her. Do you know what I'm talking about? Do you have someone like this near your life? (I say "near" because too often we let people be part of the church and yet, do not let them be part of our lives.) Over a period of several days, my wife and I spent some time with her. She wanted to be a disciple and wanted to be discipled. In all the conversations about her demeanor and her problems, no one had seemed to understand the "hell" she had to endure at home. She did not feel believed in, encouraged or understood. She's doing better now. Loving up on her did not make her sinful nature go away, but it did help the medicine of correction go down a bit easier.

Are you loving your brothers and sisters deeply from the heart? It is the "most excellent way" to live. You can speak twenty different languages, be eloquent in your challenging and persuading, but if you do not love from the heart, you are nothing more than a "resounding gong" or "clanging cymbal." If we truly love from the heart, people will know that we are disciples of Jesus Christ, the most loving of all.

LIFE APPLICATION

What have you learned specifically from Jesus about how to love deeply from the heart?

In your life, who has helped you to know Jesus by loving you deeply? Do you tend to take this person/ these people for granted, or do you express gratitude and appreciation?

List two of the "one another" teachings that are strengths in your character and two that are weaknesses. How can you use your strengths to most encourage others? How can you grow stronger in your areas of weakness?

Who in your life right now do you need to love deeply from the heart? How will you express that love?

19 Accepting One Another

BRIAN SCANLON

> Accept one another, then, just as Christ accepted you, in order to bring praise to God.
>
> Romans 15:7

"Dad, will you play with me?" "Do you think you can find a place for me in the company?" "Would you want to go out with me this Saturday night?" These are vulnerable questions that leave us open to the possibility of rejection. Most of us had experienced much rejection by the time we came into the kingdom of God, and then we felt accepted as never before. And yet, haven't we all felt unaccepted at one time or another, even in the church? Who hasn't struggled to accept a brother or sister at some point? It shouldn't surprise us, but it should make us take seriously the call of the apostle Paul to "accept one another just as Christ accepted you."

Just As Christ Accepted You

In Luke 15:11-32, the image of the father totally accepting his delinquent son speaks loudly. Before the son could finish explaining himself, he was dressed like a king and seated before a feast! That's how we've been accepted! God doesn't expect perfection, just that we're headed in the right direction with the right heart. God's acceptance is more than simply not rejecting us. It's much more than just tolerating our imperfection. It's even more than extending forgiveness. God desires to be in a relationship with us so much that when we decide to take several steps toward him, he comes running toward us and throws his arms around us. That is how we are to accept one another!

Yet, if it had been the older brother in the parable who had initially seen his brother returning, it would have been quite a different welcome. The older brother illustrates what is always the fundamental issue when we have problems accepting others: *pride.* Our pride says we can earn our place in the family of God by years of slaving away in strict obedience, which never allows us to be fully accepted by God through grace. Our pride also keeps us from accepting others until they have proven themselves, living up to some artificial standard we impose upon them. We think we're better than they are—more intelligent, more sincere, more deserving. God says in Proverbs 8:13, "I hate pride and arrogance," and we need to feel that same hatred toward our pride. It's unclear how that story ends between the two brothers, but we do know that even if the older tolerated the younger's presence, he would never have been able to accept him fully without radically changing his arrogant attitude.

Our humility is truly put to the test as we are called to accept those who are *difficult* for us to be with and those who seem very *different.* An important first step is to recognize that each of us is or has been considered difficult or different by someone at some time.

Accepting Those Who Are Difficult

The world is full of people who have lived through difficult, even horrifying, situations, and many come from those situations into the church. The fact is that some disciples just have a more difficult time than others overcoming certain sins and temptations. Years of brutality can twist the personality and destroy the character of people to the point that some of us have a hard time accepting them. I'm not talking about making excuses for people or tolerating unrepentant sin, but rather about being patient with people and showing compassion. We can become so concerned that others don't take advantage of grace that we no longer extend it. The "three strikes and you're out" approach just is not going to work in the kingdom. If we are not careful, in our efforts to make hard-line disciples, we may end up making hard-hearted ones, unwilling to bear with the weaknesses of others. It's too easy to distance ourselves from others, making superficial judgments without really knowing what is going on in their lives.

I remember several years ago seeing someone in fellowship who seemed far more aloof "than a disciple of Jesus should be," and decided that we needed to have a strong talk. He recounted years of physical, emotional and sexual abuse by family and friends. Though he was aware of the effects of sin on his personality and wanted to change, he often didn't know how to change and lacked faith in himself. It was very clear that this change was not going to happen overnight. In the meantime, he did not need to be looked down upon as a second-class Christian. He needed to be accepted. And in the months to come he became a fruitful part of the ministry.

Accepting Those Who Are Different

Coming to Paris to build the church was one of the greatest challenges in my life. At the time, a naive American who had never lived in another country, I found myself surrounded by people who often saw things differently than I did. In most cases it had nothing to do with right or wrong; we just had different tastes and opinions. However, it was only recently that the greatest challenge came my way: My wife began to study the Bible with a single woman who had undergone a sex-change operation. Upon learning of this situation, I was stunned, to put it kindly. In France, people greet each other with a kiss on each cheek, and I am ashamed of what I felt the first time I met her. However, my self-righteous pride melted as I watched her come to understand the seriousness of what she had done in God's eyes and face what were, for many reasons, the irreparable consequences of her sin. The day of her baptism, I made sure that I was one of the first to wholeheartedly welcome her into the kingdom of God. Because of our acceptance of each other in spite of our differences, God has worked powerfully over the past six years to build a richly diverse church, worthy of the great cosmopolitan city of Paris.

In a world where people are held captive by the fear of rejection, the church of Jesus Christ must be a place where we accept one another as he has accepted us. This brings praise and glory to God in the church!

LIFE APPLICATION

Have you fully accepted the grace of God or are you still trying to earn it?

Is there anyone in the church that you find difficult to be with—anyone that you have not accepted? How will you go about repenting and changing your attitude?

Make a list of types of people you might find it most difficult to accept. Then think through how you believe Jesus would treat each of them.

Do you feel unaccepted by anyone in the church? If so, get advice from someone who is spiritually wise as to the best way to approach this person or this situation.

20 Devoted to One Another

DEBBIE MCDANIEL

Be devoted to one another in brotherly love.

Romans 12:10

The Internet. The World Wide Web. America Online. Compuserve. Cyberspace. Our world is rapidly progressing to a point where deep, devoted relationships are being exchanged for association through a computer screen and a keyboard. As our technology grows, so does the distance in heart-to-heart communication. Our generation is afraid, protective, distrusting and consumed with self. The days of unlocked doors at night, a sense of family in our neighborhoods and friendship without a hidden agenda are quickly disappearing. Every day we read in our newspapers about another murder, rape or abusive episode perpetrated by a friend or relative. Teen suicide and teen pregnancy are at an all-time high. The number of children being raised in a two-parent home is at an all-time low.

It is time for the kingdom of God to shine brighter than ever before! In today's society it is crucial that disciples model deep, committed and devoted relationships. Our world needs us, and our God is counting on us. Obviously, we will neither be perfect nor have relationships that are without conflict. But the power of the kingdom is demonstrated when men and women, who would have possibly been enemies and strangers in this world, give up their prejudices and make a decision to die to themselves so that they can "love each other deeply from the heart"(1 Peter 1:22).

Romans 12:10 calls us to be devoted to one another in "brotherly love." The Greek here is refering to the love and commitment that is found in family relationships. How bright is the light when the world sees us not just loving each other and living in harmony, but living in familial devotion to one another—as true brothers and sisters. As the world around us watches the family unit slowly decaying and dying, we can show the whole world God's power and God's love through our devotion to each other. Isn't that the way Jesus meant it to be? (See John 13:35.)

Take It Higher!

But even in the kingdom, we need to take it much higher. Through my years as a disciple, I have seen and helped many women make the decision to take on the lordship of Jesus in baptism. However, I have also seen many make the decision to leave Jesus, his kingdom and their brothers and sisters. They no longer have a respect for God or his word. Some make a decision to go back to the world and return to their sin even after much pleading and tears from those who love them. But others, after entering the kingdom and expecting it to be different from the world around them, leave because they have not been cared for, loved and understood. They came in expecting family and found superficial friendship. They did not experience the devotion that would carry them through thick and thin.

I know that I would not be here today if my sisters during my early years as a disciple had not poured out their lives for me. They were truly living out Philippians 2:3-4 in considering my interests more important than their own. The late-night telephone calls, the long walks and talks, the pouring out of our hearts together in prayer, the ongoing Bible studies after my baptism, the cards, the daily love and care...all showed me that we were sisters. We helped each other make it through the painful, troubling times along the way. We worked and struggled together so we would all make it home to see our Father in heaven. Even today, we would do anything for each other as we serve in the kingdom of our God all over the world.

Serve from the Heart

In 1987, shortly before Kevin and I entered the full-time ministry, the selfishness in my heart began to expose itself. Outwardly I was doing all of the right things: serving, loving, having people in my home, giving rides, babysitting, etc. But my life was not really making an impact on my sisters or on the world around me. I did not feel deeply bonded with my sisters;

yet I would say, of course, that I loved them. Even though I had made a decision many years before to stop living for myself and to live for Jesus, I had begun again to live for me, even as a disciple. I had stopped giving my heart and my life away.

Reality hit home when, on my twenty-seventh birthday, no one remembered or even sent me a card—not even my best friend. Instead of responding angrily or bitterly, I stopped and asked myself, "Why should they? What difference have I really made in their lives?" Was I really living as though others' interests were more important than my own? Or did I meet the needs of those around me only when it was convenient and comfortable? I saw the telephone as burdensome at times and wondered if it would ever stop ringing. But my heart was quickly cut as I read and studied Jesus' heart in John 12:24-26:

> "I tell you the truth, unless a kernel of wheat falls to the ground and dies, it remains only a single seed. But if it dies, it produces many seeds. The man who loves his life will lose it, while the man who hates his life in this world will keep it for eternal life. Whoever serves me must follow me."

I realized that the deep devotion that I needed for my brothers and sisters was getting squelched by my love for myself.

As I studied through relationships like those of David and Jonathan, Ruth and Naomi, Paul and Timothy, I saw what was still lacking in my life and heart, and I made decisions about being radically different. I repented and nine months later entered the full-time ministry with my husband! Sometimes I look back on the person I was in 1987 and wonder if she was really me. God has truly transformed my life and heart so that I can make a difference in this world and have deep, meaningful relationships. Yet, the spiritual battle still rages. Each day we must overcome the temptation to live for ourselves and resolve instead to be radically "devoted to one another."

LIFE APPLICATION

When you hear the word "devoted," who immediately comes to your mind? What lessons about being devoted do you most need to learn from them?

What do you fear most about being completely devoted to others? With whom will you share those fears this week?

Do you feel people in the family of God have been devoted to you? Suppose the answer is no. Would that change what God wants you to show to others? How could an experience of not feeling loved be turned into something positive?

Why do actions have more impact in demonstrating devotion than just words? What actions will you take this week that will speak louder than words?

21 Greeting One Another

SHEILA JONES

Greet one another with a holy kiss. All the churches of Christ send greetings.

Romans 16:16

When we enter a room, probably nothing warms our hearts more than being greeted by a toddler who knows us. The outstretched arms, wide eyes and squeals of delight make us feel like the most loved and most important person in the world at that moment. You see, a toddler has not yet learned to "tone down" his responses. He has not been schooled in being cool. He doesn't worry about causing others to feel so special that his own specialness is threatened. A toddler has the heart that Jesus calls us all to have in Matthew 18:3-4.

When the Scripture tells us again and again to greet each other with a holy kiss (Romans 16:16; 2 Corinthians 13:12; 1 Thessalonians 5:26; 1 Peter 5:14), God is saying, Let your brothers and sisters know that they are special, that you are happy to see them. In essence, God does not want us to treat as routine something that is precious in his eyes: the relationships in his ransomed family bought by the blood of his only Son.

Sin Makes Us Aloof

Why do we sometimes not greet each other "warmly in the Lord" as Aquila and Priscilla greeted the Corinthian church? (See 1 Corinthians 16:19.) Maybe we can get a clue by observing the people in a certain Samaritan village who did not welcome Jesus "because he was heading for Jerusalem" (Luke 9:53). They were resentful of the Jews who were traveling through their country to the Holy City to participate in exclusive religious feasts, refusing them lodging on their three-day journey. They did not welcome Jesus or greet him warmly because they had attitudes of resentment, bitterness, jealousy, pride and arrogance to name a few. Could it be that our own sinful attitudes bar us from greeting others warmly, from giving our hearts immediately? Could we add self-focus, fear of rejection and lack of love to the list of wall-building, coolness-engendering sins?

Believe it or not, the way we welcome or greet others in a public or private setting reflects our attitude toward God himself. Jesus said, "Whoever welcomes one of these little children in my name welcomes me; and whoever welcomes me does not welcome me but the one who sent me" (Mark 9:37). If we are thankful to God for showering us with grace, we will be grateful for the family of believers who share in that grace. We will be vulnerable, not aloof. We will be warm, not cool. We will welcome others "with great joy" evident in our hearts (Philippians 2:29).

Prepare for Greeting Others

Praying for people affects the way we greet them. When they are on our hearts and minds, we are at once happy to see them. At a worship service, our hearts will not need the spiritual massage of lively singing to finally wake up and greet someone. They will sense our enthusiasm and support when our eyes first meet. Paul told the Colossians,

> Epaphras, who is one of you and a servant of Christ Jesus, sends greetings. He is always wrestling in prayer for you, that you may stand firm in all the will of God, mature and fully assured (Colossians 4:12).

His greeting was motivated by his prayerful awareness of those whom he loved. Of course, when we go to a service, we cannot have prayed for everyone we will greet, but we need to have on our hearts specifically the people God has placed in our everyday lives. They are our main connections to the rest of the family. And if our hearts go out quickly to them, our warmth will draw others in along the way. The truth about warmth is that it radiates in many directions, not only in the direction it is aimed.

Take It to Heart

Since I began to write this chapter, I have been thinking more about the way I greet people. I tend to take people for granted and become rather business-like. I want warm greetings to be a hallmark of my character, but for that to happen, I must die to my selfishness. When I am not enthusiastic in greeting others, it is generally because I am too concerned about Sheila: what she is feeling, what all she has to do. Certainly I expect others to greet me warmly and be out of themselves and make me feel loved. What I need to do is to turn the camera on me, to become first aware of my own self-centeredness and pride, and then to become more aware of others' need to feel loved and special.

I began to mentally scroll through my list of friends, considering who was especially warm and encouraging in their greetings. One who came to mind was Lori Bynum, a women's ministry leader in the Boston area. I don't believe that anyone offers warmer greetings than Lori. Like the toddler mentioned earlier, she makes me feel that I am the most important person in the world in the moment of her greeting. We have known each other for years, and yet she never treats me as "old hat" or like last night's meat loaf (good, but nothing special). And what is so encouraging is this: She makes everyone she greets feel "most important" in that moment.

I called a woman with whom Lori works in the ministry and asked her to respond to the question, "How does Lori make you feel when she greets you?"

She first spoke of Lori's incredible, contagious smile. Then she said, "Lori always reaches out a hand or an arm to touch or hug me. Her tone communicates her excitement to see me, as does her expression and the twinkle in her eye. She always asks, 'How are you doing?' and means it."

When we greet each other, whether we give a holy kiss or just give a quick hug, let's make each other feel special, because in our Father's eyes, we are all just that—very special.

LIFE APPLICATION

How would others generally characterize your greetings: (1) distracted and cool or (2) warm and engaging?

How does your closeness or lack of closeness with God affect your relationships with your brothers and sisters?

How often do you think about how to make others feel special when you first see them? If everyone in your group greeted each other just as you do, what would be the tone of the fellowship?

What commitment will you make to change the nature of your greetings?

22 Carrying Each Other's Burdens

DAVE MALUTINOK
Atlanta, Georgia

Brothers, if someone is caught in a sin, you who are spiritual should restore him gently. But watch yourself, or you also may be tempted. Carry each other's burdens, and in this way you will fulfill the law of Christ.

Galatians 6:1-2

Paul was serious about people not sinning. He was also serious about spiritual people taking the responsibility to restore gently those who were "caught in a sin." In Galatians 5:19-20 he clearly defined sin; then in verses 22-26 he described the fruit of the Spirit. His heart's desire was that the disciples not "become conceited, provoking or envying each other" (5:26), but that they watch out for each other and carry each other's burden of sin. As we drift away from God's truth, it takes someone spiritual to see our hardness of heart, to confront our sin, and bring us back to the truth.

Seeing the Burden

We can easily see physical burdens such as the loss of a job or a death in the family. While we are unquestionably called to carry physical burdens for each other, taken in context, Galatians 6:1-2 concerns itself more with carrying spiritual burdens—i.e. restoring a brother's or sister's soft heart. It is usually much more difficult to carry spiritual burdens because they are not as apparent as the physical ones. To see spiritual burdens requires openness in the one who is burdened, and spiritual insight in the one who confronts and helps to carry that burden.

Why does Paul single out those "who are spiritual" to be the ones to restore the burdened disciple? It is the precedent set by Jesus in Luke 6:42, where he says,

"How can you say to your brother, 'Brother, let me take the speck out of your eye,' when you yourself fail to see the plank in your own eye? You hypocrite, first take the plank out of your eye, and then you will see clearly to remove the speck from your brother's eye."

The truly humble person who sees his own faults is also the truly spiritual person.

Many times I am tempted to be critical and find fault in others. Through discipling, I have learned that when I feel critical, or feel as though I see some glaring faults, I first must look at my own heart. *Am I being righteous? Is there a plank in my own eye?* If I do have a plank, Jesus says I will not see clearly—my spiritual insight is tainted with my own sin. I then realize that I must keep silent, pray and repent of that plank in my own eye. Once I've allowed God to take the plank out, I will see clearly to find the speck in the eye of my brother.

Have you ever wondered why some people are so insightful? You may be completely unaware of a spiritual burden that someone else can pick up on immediately. I believe insight comes from a deep relationship with God. To be able to see the spiritual burdens in our brothers and sisters, we must walk closely with God.

Restoring the Brother

The Greek word used by Paul which is translated "restore" means "to restore as to set a broken bone." Further, the Greek meaning for "carry," found in Galatians 6:2, means "to take the weight of another person's load." While in Boston, I had the painful opportunity to understand the literal meaning of these two words.

Jim Lenahen and I joined the local YMCA, where we hoped to build relationships playing basketball with the "lunch crowd." On our first day, we were warming up with a game of "one-on-one" while we waited for the other players. On my first shot, we both went up for the rebound; Jim landed first, and I landed on the top of his foot. We heard a loud "crack," which was followed by severe pain in my ankle. There was no doubt about it—I had broken my ankle.

Two things had to happen: First, someone had to pull my foot to set my ankle back into its proper position. When a trainer and Jim performed the procedure, the pain was excruciating! But once my bone was restored, it began feeling better. Second, I had to be carried off the court. Because of the weakness of my newly restored bone, I could not put any weight on it. Therefore, Jim bore my weight on his ankles.

I think you can see the spiritual parallel to this story. When we sin, we need to be restored. But to be restored is painful (Hebrews 12:5-11). Yet, we must go through that pain, or we will never heal.

It also helped that I had a relationship with Jim. I knew he would watch out for me in my weakness. I knew that I had to go through the pain of setting my ankle, and because of our relationship, I trusted Jim's judgment.

Because of his love for me, Jim could not let me lie there in pain. His first thought was to carry my full weight on his body, because I couldn't carry my weight on my own. When someone is caught in a sin, will you let him or her lie on the "court" in agony, or will you set the spiritual broken bone and carry them? Is your heart's desire is to protect them and allow them to heal?

Fulfilling the Law

When we see the sin and spiritual burden of our brother and then, with wisdom and gentleness, restore him to health, Paul said we fulfill the law (or principle) of Christ!

In John 13:35, Jesus tells the disciples that they are to love each other as he had loved them: a kind of love that restores the soul and carries that soul's burden. Loving each other in this way will be the proof to all mankind that Jesus is the Son of God and that we are part of his glorious church on earth.

How insightful are you in noticing the spiritual burdens of your close friends?

What can cause you to be insensitive to others' burdens?

What is your greatest fear in helping someone who is "caught in a sin"? What decision will you make to overcome this fear?

Think of a time when someone restored you when you were trapped and broken by sin. Especially in light of your answer to the question above, how appreciative are you of this person?

23 Speaking the Truth in Love

JEANIE SHAW
Glastonbury, Connecticut

> Then we will no longer be infants, tossed back and forth by the waves, and blown here and there by every wind of teaching and by the cunning and craftiness of men in their deceitful scheming. Instead, speaking the truth in love, we will in all things grow up into him who is the Head, that is, Christ.
>
> Ephesians 4:14-15

This chapter is for all conflict avoiders. I had to laugh when I received this topic because speaking the truth has been so hard for me. Conflict avoidance runs deep in my sinful nature. Sinful...because it is a sin not to speak the truth in order to avoid conflict. At this point in my life, though it is often difficult, God is making me strong where I am weak.

I can remember an instance in kindergarten when I ran away from school and hid in my garage rather than tell my teacher that I had forgotten my lunch money! Later in life, my college roommate was designated "Martyr of the Month" in my dorm because I had spoken the truth to her about God. I had come a long way from hiding in the garage.

After I was married and was serving full-time in the ministry, I gently shared with an older woman what I believed the younger women in the congregation needed her to be as a role model. The next thing I knew, she was upset, her husband was upset and my husband was fired.

Then, somewhere along the way, I lost my conviction and courage and instead of speaking the truth in love, I started stuffing the truth in fear.

Stuffing the Truth in Fear

Jesus is truth. He was known, even as the Pharisees tried to trap him in his words, as a man of integrity and a man of truth. "Teacher, we know you are a man of integrity. You aren't swayed by men, because you pay no attention to who they are;

but you teach the way of God in accordance with the truth" (Mark 12:14).

Jesus was a man of deep conviction. His convictions were based on God's truth, not on other people's opinions. How often do we stuff the truth because we are afraid of what people will think of us or how they will react? I feared people's reactions so much that I learned a common stuffing technique. I would subconsciously reason that *I should not* feel or think a certain thing so therefore *I would not.* I learned to deny feelings rather than be open with them.

Speak the Truth to Everyone

Speaking the truth in love applies to all of our life situations. First, we must learn to speak the truth to ourselves. Sometimes, we deny what we really think, even in our own hearts and minds. We can also react defensively to others, to the Bible or to a sermon. Insecurity and pride often keep us from welcoming the truth into our hearts. Do you make it easy for others to speak the truth to you?

Second, we must speak the truth to our brothers and sisters. Unresolved attitudes bring about deceit, bitterness and slander. When we have quiet reservations about someone's motives and assume the worst, Satan wins. Jesus loved his friends enough to bring things into the light. He went beyond the shallow conversation and into the attitudes of the heart. "What were you arguing about on the road?" Jesus asked his disciples in Mark 9:33. He set us an example in being direct and speaking to the heart.

Third, we must love the lost enough to speak the truth to them. Jesus spoke to a man who "had it all" in Mark 10. Verse 21 simply states, "Jesus looked at him and loved him." He proved his love by speaking the truth about how the man could inherit eternal life. Do we see others through Jesus' eyes of compassion? No matter what is on the outside, without spiritual truth we are all helpless and harassed, like sheep without a shepherd.

Love Is a Safe Place

In order to "speak the truth in love," it helps to know that "in love" is a safe place. I found it hard to be vulnerable until I learned that the unconditional love in the kingdom of God is a safe place. There was a time in my life when I had a lot of hurt feelings and attitudes toward another disciple. I didn't want to have these feelings, so I pretended I didn't. I was afraid to express them honestly. A brother asked me if I believed I was in a safe place in the kingdom of God. The tears flowed as I saw the beauty of God's plan. I spoke the truth and the sister and I ended up closer than ever.

Speaking the truth in love is always for the purpose of building up. Perhaps much of the fear often associated with speaking the truth would be alleviated if we made a daily effort to encourage one another on the truth about the good things. This, too, is a significant part of speaking the truth in love. It does not only mean talking about conflict and hard teachings. The truth also consists of whatever is noble, right, pure, lovely, admirable, excellent or praiseworthy (Philippians 4:8).

Time to Grow Up

Conviction about God's word, planted deep in our hearts and flowing freely from our mouths, is the means by which we grow from infants into grown-ups. If we stuff the truth in fear, we will vacillate between what everyone else thinks and what we know is true; and we will know in our heart of hearts that we are being cowards.

However, when we hold firmly to the truth, and love God and others enough to express it, "we will no longer be infants, tossed back and forth by the waves....Instead, speaking the truth in love, we will in all things grow up into him who is the Head, that is, Christ" (Ephesians 4:14-15).

LIFE APPLICATION

Can you think of a time when you, in love, shared the truth about someone's sin with him or her and the response was not encouraging? How did you let it affect you?

In speaking the truth in love, are you known as being an encourager like Barnabas and a refresher like Onesiphorus?

How consistently do you notice and point out the good and the growth in those around you? If a word were placed by your name to describe your character toward others, what would it be?

When you have something difficult to say, are you direct or do you beat around the bush? Why is it always better to be direct but kind?

24 Submitting to One Another

KELLY PETRE
Albuquerque, New Mexico

Submit to one another out of reverence for Christ.
Ephesians 5:21

Jesus, the pre-existent Word, "was with God, and the Word was God" (John 1:1-2). Yet, that same Word, "being in very nature God, did not consider equality with God something to be grasped, but...being made in human likeness...he humbled himself and became obedient" (Philippians 2:6-8).

Jesus, the 12-year-old boy, sat among teachers in the temple, amazing his listeners with a wisdom beyond his years. This same boy-wonder left for Nazareth with his parents and "was obedient to them" (Luke 2:51).

Jesus, the sinless one, approached an astonished John the Baptist. John protested, "I need to be baptized by you, and do you come to me?" But Jesus persuaded him that "it is proper to do this to fulfill all righteousness" (Matthew 3:14-15) and was baptized by John.

Jesus, the Son of God, almost got stoned to death proclaiming himself "one with the Father" (John 10:30-33) and, yet, persisted in his claim so that "the world might learn that I love the Father and that I do exactly what my Father has commanded" (John 14:31).

Jesus, the miracle worker, was impressed by a non-Jew pleading for the health of his servant. The Roman centurion revealed more than belief that Jesus could heal at a distance when he declared, "I myself am a man under authority, with soldiers under me" (Luke 7:8). His experiences had given him great understanding as to the right application of authority and the power of submission.

Jesus, the leader, proclaimed himself "Teacher and Lord" (John 13:13), but commanded his followers to imitate his example as he humbly washed their dirty feet.

Jesus, the sacrificial lamb, "offered up prayers and petitions with loud cries and tears to the one who could save him from death," but because he was reverently submissive, "he learned obedience" (Hebrews 5:7-8) as Roman soldiers drove spikes through his hands and feet.

What amazing contrasts stand out in the life of this man! Jesus Christ, the Lord of all, to whom all must submit, was also Jesus Christ, humble and obedient servant, submissive to parents, to followers, to government and to God. So powerful— yet so willing to submit!

In All Our Relationships

Christianity is relationships. As followers of Christ, we learn from his example what attitude we are to have in those relationships. Because we revere Christ as Lord, a submissive spirit must always characterize our hearts. Whether these relationships occur between wives and husbands, children and parents, slaves and masters (students and teachers, employees and bosses), citizens and government, or church members and church leaders, we are to submit *to* the roles we are called to fulfill and submit *in* those roles accordingly. What is more, a humble and submissive spirit must reign even in those to whom authority is given as we submit to one another.

I am continually in awe of the results of submission as it is practiced and lived out in Jesus' church. What joyful marriages! What strong families! What an attractive work ethic! What unbelievable growth worldwide! Never have I seen more abundant evidence that God's way is right. What a striking difference from following our "natural" inclinations to be prideful, independent, arrogant and selfish!

Although this principle applies to all of our relationships, it certainly has special significance for our discipling relationships. Without submitting to one another in discipling relationships, there can be no glory in the church. You see, our own spiritual growth, as well as the evangelization of the world, depends on our becoming like Christ. The first key to becoming like Christ is a deep personal desire to walk as he did. The second key is to disciple one another to maturity in Christ. Discipling requires a willingness to to lay down our lives and to love others enough to teach, to correct, to rebuke, to encourage and to train. It also requires the willingness and eagerness to be taught, corrected, rebuked, encouraged and disciplined. In short, without voluntary submission, discipling cannot occur. And without discipling, Christlikeness will never occur.

New Pages of Submission

For the first six years of my Christian walk I was discipled by the same man. As a non-Christian, I just wanted to be like him. As a Christian, he loved, challenged, molded and taught me. Perhaps one of the hardest times for me spiritually was the day he moved to become part of a different ministry. What now? Surely no one could replace him in my life! A special brother helped me see that it wasn't an issue of anyone or anything replacing what I'd had in the past. Rather, it was time to "turn the page" and begin a new chapter in my life. "Acts 1 was pretty good," he grinned, "but Acts 2 wasn't bad either!" And he was right—boy, was he right! You see, as long as we remain faithful to God and submissive to his plan of discipleship, our best days are never in the past!

In the six years since that time I have been discipled by nearly a dozen different men. I have been in many different ministries and have surrendered many different dreams as I have "turned the page" from Paris to Boston to Toronto to Montreal to Boston again. With each new discipleship partner, I have had to decide all over again to give my heart fully to the one God has placed in my life. The differing strengths of each of these brothers have inspired and called me higher. I have also learned many lessons from peers and from those men I have discipled along the way. I have been the winner every time!

Every leader God puts in our lives is different. There are challenges and blessings unique to every friendship. But it is a privilege to be discipled by anyone. We must *decide* to have a willing heart, to be eager to learn, to be open to input and direction and to have a submissive attitude toward the particular person that God has placed in our lives to help us to be more like Christ.

Look to Jesus, and follow his example. Out of reverence for him, let us submit to one another in all areas of our lives!

LIFE APPLICATION

As God in the flesh, Jesus was certainly no weakling. What does his example teach you about the nature of submission? What does it teach you that submission is *not*?

How Christlike is your submission in the following relationships (wife/husband, child/parent, student/teacher, employee/boss, citizen/government, church member/church leaders)? How Christlike is your use of authority?

How willing and submissive is your heart toward your discipler? What are you learning from him or her?

List what you stand to gain or lose by being submissive in your relationships. Then list what is gained or lost by not being submissive. Which makes more sense?

25 Admonishing and Teaching One Another

MIKE FONTENOT
Australia

We proclaim him, admonishing and teaching everyone with all wisdom, so that we may present everyone perfect in Christ.
Colossians 1:28

Let the word of Christ dwell in you richly as you teach and admonish one another with all wisdom, and as you sing psalms, hymns and spiritual songs with gratitude in your hearts to God.
Colossians 3:16

Fatherhood is one of life's biggest challenges. It is glorious and rewarding; it is frustrating and confusing. Yet Paul instructs fathers in that difficult situation to be careful not to "exasperate" their children! Instead, they are to "bring them up in the training and instruction of the Lord" (Ephesians 6:4). The language is quite similar to the text "to teach and admonish one another." In fact the word "instruction" is the same Greek word *noutheteo* that is translated "admonish." Actually, raising up children and raising up each other have many similarities. Teaching and admonishing are two sides of the same coin—both are essential for all of us to grow up into the likeness of Christ.

Let's consider three keys to bringing each other to maturity and bringing glory to God in his church.

Teach and Admonish

"Teach" is from the Greek word *didasko*, from the root word *dek*, which conveys the idea of repeatedly extending the hand for acceptance. It denotes the concept of helping someone over and over again to understand and to accept what you are saying. Teaching is communicating the facts and information so that the student understands. It is getting the student's mind and intellect to grasp what the Bible says and to comprehend how it all fits together. Good teaching makes very plain the deeper subjects such as Christ, the cross and the Christian life (2 Timothy 2:15). Good teaching produces a solid foundation for the life of a disciple. It increases trust in God because we clearly understand what the Bible is calling us to do and to be. It is easier to obey if we understand!

"Admonish" is from the Greek word *noutheteo* derived from *nous* (mind) and *tithemi* (put). It describes the effort to change the other's will, to put the teaching on the mind. In contrast to *didasko*, which concerns the intellect, *noutheteo* has to do with the will and feelings of a person. It is very possible for us to know what we need to do, yet at the same time make little or no effort to actually do it. Admonishing is taking the knowledge learned from teaching and insisting that those truths be actually lived. It is going deeper than just "I agree" to a point where the heart is changed and deeds follow. This is not winning a debate where all arguments are silenced with no intention of obedience. Admonishing is changing the will, removing hidden reservations and affecting the heart. In my religious past, there was never a shortage of knowledge but rather a dearth of action. Judaism in Paul's day produced exactly the same results.

With All Wisdom

Paul goes further in adding to both passages that teaching and admonishing must be done with all wisdom. This has more to do with how we say things rather than what we have to say. Paul illustrates this while visiting the Ephesian elders in Acts 20. He reminds them that he warned (*noutheteo*) them day and night with tears (v31), most likely their tears and his tears. Tears often demonstrate the depth of concern and love for each other. Our hearts hurt as we deal with anyone who understands yet will not act on those convictions. And tears are often the needed "drink offering" that shows the other person we really do care. In many situations people do not listen until tears come and voices break with emotion.

In addition to tears, wisdom included the individual effort Paul made with *each* of them. Paul did not just publicly preach it and hope they got it. He got down eyeball to eyeball to make sure that what was taught was understood, agreed upon and put into practice. "With all wisdom" never loses sight of the goal—maturity in Christ. It is not about power or winning an argument or making a point. It is about helping the other disciple be transformed into the image of Christ.

Atmosphere of Respect

Lastly, for great "teaching and admonishing" to be fostered, there needs to be an atmosphere of respect. "Respect those who work hard among you, who are over you in the Lord and who *admonish* you"(1 Thessalonians 5:12, emphasis added). The Greek word for respect, *eido*, is "to pay attention, to have regard for the other." We need to desire input and to be attentive when we do receive it. In fact, we need to love input. Although it sometimes hurts, it helps us to become mature. As with child-rearing, it is often only really understood when we become parents and realize what our parents did for us. Likewise, as we start raising others up, we realize what tremendous sacrifice and effort was made on our behalf to bring us to maturity. And the proper response is respect for those who ventured into our lives to help us grow.

How do you show respect? Ask for input rather than waiting defensively to get it. Respond openly, and help others help you. Don't just sit there and stare. Pray that the Lord will send others into your life to help you. Share with others the input you have received and what you are trying to change in your life. Be honest about the tender, sensitive spots that need healing. And finally, show respect by treating the instructor and the instruction you receive with appreciation.

To "teach and admonish one another" is an essential, indispensable activity that is required for us to be raised to maturity. The wise know that the input never ends and, thankfully, that the growing is never over.

LIFE APPLICATION

How patient are you when trying to teach someone a concept difficult for them to understand? What motivates you to be patient?

Why does it take great energy for you to teach someone—and even more to admonish them? What forces work against their understanding and accepting? What role should prayer play in this process? What role does it actually play in your life?

Do you cry or show emotion easily when you admonish a stubborn person? Do you cry out of your own frustration or out of love for the person?

Do you ask for input so you can grow, or do you defensively wait for it? Who will you talk to about growing in this area?

26 Encouraging One Another Daily

THERESA FERGUSON
McKenney, Texas

> But encourage one another daily, as long as it is called Today,
> so that none of you may be hardened by sin's deceitfulness.
> Hebrews 3:13

If I were to ask the question, "Who needs to be encouraged?" the unanimous answer would be "everyone" (especially *me*!). Yes, we all need copious amounts of it, but it is also a command of God for every disciple to be an encourager. We tend to look to leaders and mature disciples for encouragement, without realizing that the newest disciple has the same responsibility. Encouragement is not something we wait expectantly to receive—it is something we expect to *give* to others. And as with all spiritual qualities, it is more blessed to give than to receive them. We feel encouraged when we give encouragement!

When does God expect us to be encouragers, to put courage into others? In a word, *daily*. The hard part is to keep it on our hearts in a way that motivates us to practice it daily. Our selfish nature makes us much more conscious of our own need to be encouraged than of our need to give encouragement. The key to victory in this area is to first get encouragement from our time with God, for only then do we have something to share. Then, we seek to imitate Jesus, learning to daily spur others on to victory.

Why did God give such a command in the first place? Hebrews 3:12-14 provides us with some great reasons. Encouragement prevents disciples from developing a "sinful, unbelieving heart that turns away from the living God," and it ensures "that none of you may be hardened by sin's deceitfulness." We are thus enabled to "hold firmly till the end the confidence we had at first." Encouragement is our weapon against Satan as we use God's promises to help each other fend off schemes designed to weaken and destroy. We are instruments of God (Romans 6:13) to be the heart-lifters, faith-instillers and spiritual-inspirers for his children. Our effectiveness is guaranteed by the Encourager (*parakletos*) given to us at baptism, the Holy Spirit.

Becoming Excellent Encouragers

How can we all become excellent encouragers? Romans 12:8 tells us that encouragement is a special gift given to certain people by the Spirit. Thus, we need to seek out and imitate those who excel in this gift. Those who have it are readily recognizable:

- *Encouragers focus on God.* They see life from the perspective of an all-powerful, all-loving God, not from the limitations of mortal men. As John put it in 1 John 4:4, "The one who is within you is greater than the one who is in the world."

- *Encouragers are great listeners.* They want to hear what is in your heart rather than dispense pat answers. They want to listen to your words and your feelings. All of us should simply strive to be like God, for he is the greatest listener of all (Psalm 10:17-18).

- *Encouragers are genuine and specific in their praise of others.* Flattery may appear appealing, but it has no lasting effect. A real encourager explains why you can be victorious and helps you learn to think about your life with God's perspective.

- *Encouragers are aware of the needs of others others and initiate to meet those needs.* I remember a number of my hospitalizations through the years when the sight of a familiar face lifted my heart like nothing else could. I remember times when I felt overwhelmed by too many chores and too little time to do them. Then a knock came at the door. When I opened it, I was met by a smiling, unexpected angel with rubber gloves and a bucket in her hands. Paul must have felt similar emotions when the brothers went to great lengths to encourage him as he traveled to Rome as a prisoner. Acts 28:15 reads:

> The brothers there had heard that we were coming, and they traveled as far as the Forum of Appius and the Three Taverns to

meet us. At the sight of these men Paul thanked God and was encouraged.

- *Encouragers are sacrificial.* The example of Barnabas, whose name meant "Son of Encouragement," demonstrates this point well. We first meet him in Acts 4:36-37 when he sells a field and gives the money to meet the needs of his brothers and sisters. Just imagine what gratitude those early disciples must have felt for Barnabas!

- *Encouragers have great vision for others.* Again, Barnabas provides us with a powerful example. After Paul's conversion he visited Jerusalem, only to discover that Jesus' apostles were afraid of him. However, it was Barnabas who persuaded them to accept Paul (Acts 9:26-27). Later, Barnabas brought him to help evangelize Samaria (Acts 11:25-26). No doubt his acceptance and encouragement of Paul had much to do with the amazingly effective apostle he became!

- *Encouragers are not sentimental or overly protective.* Peter did not encourage Jesus when he tried to persuade him not to go to the cross (Matthew 16:22-23), no matter how noble his intentions may have seemed. True biblical encouragement points others in the direction of the cross, which by its nature is not easy. Paul and Barnabas dispensed help by "strengthening the disciples and encouraging them to remain true to the faith. 'We must go through many hardships to enter the kingdom of God,' they said" (Acts 14:22).

- *Encouragers offer hope to others by sharing openly from their own lives.* Nothing encourages others quite like being allowed into the hearts and lives of those offering help. Hearing about past defeats and victories of the presently strong imparts tremendous hope to those who are presently weak.

Let us set our hearts on becoming a great encourager of other people. Then on the Day of Judgment, many will rise up to call us blessed. When we have imitated those like Jesus, Paul and Barnabas, we will produce this heart-warming response in those whom we seek to encourage: "I am greatly encouraged; in all our troubles my joy knows no bounds" (2 Corinthians 7:4).

LIFE APPLICATION

From the article, pick out your strongest points as an encourager and your weakest points. Share your findings with someone who knows you well, and ask their opinion about your answers.

How well do you accept encouragement from others? What keeps you from accepting it better? (Think about your pride, independence, etc.)

What types of things typically cause you to become discouraged?

What have others done that encouraged you the most?

How can you tell when others need to be encouraged?

27 Spurring One Another On

TERRIE FONTENOT
Australia

> And let us consider how we may spur one another on toward love and good deeds. Let us not give up meeting together, as some are in the habit of doing, but let us encourage one another—and all the more as you see the Day approaching.
> Hebrews 10:24-25

Motivation! Performance! Productivity! These are concepts that the whole world is interested in, as evidenced by the large number of articles, books and seminars on the topics. Yet long before any humanistic motivational materials were produced, God himself saw and spoke to the need for groups to be motivated to become more productive. In our theme passage the writer commands us to think about how we can motivate one another to a greater performance of love and good deeds in the church.

Why?

The account of a first-century tax collector is a perfect example of how the love of Christ is our basic motivation to love and perform good deeds. Zacchaeus responded whole-heartedly to Jesus' love by quadrupling the repayment of his debt (Luke 19:1-10). Paul puts forth the same idea in 2 Corinthians 5:14 when he writes "For Christ's love compels us, because we are convinced that one died for all, and therefore all died." Clearly, our motivation to spur one another on to good deeds is the love that Jesus has freely given to each of us.

How?

Having established our motivation, "let us consider how we may spur one another on toward love and good deeds." The challenge here is *to think*, and some of our best thinking comes in the form of prayer. The Spirit helps us to have insight into people's lives and to know how to help them. As we pray, God will give us ideas that will strengthen and encourage individuals or the church as a whole.

The idea of "spurring" someone on is really considering how you can provoke them or stir them up. If you have ever watched a cowboy movie, you realize that when the rider spurs the horse, there is a slight pain inflicted followed by immediate action on the part of the horse. We all become complacent and lazy at times in our spiritual lives and thus we are all commanded to "spur" each other on or "put the boot in" as they say in Australia.

In fact, in verse 25 the author tells us that disciples can become so dull that they even stop meeting together. Maybe it is not our habit to miss church, but we can violate this scripture and still be present because the admonishment is not just to be there, but to "encourage one another." There is a sense of urgency in this verse to be encouraging, to help others have courage to do what is right. The time God has given us in the fellowship is to prepare each other for eternity.

Specifics

Here are some things to consider in order to spur one another along in the fellowship:

- Have eyes that watch the flock. Look for those who are sad or troubled. Go directly to those people with the purpose of encouraging and spurring them on. During your prayer time on Sunday morning and on the way to the service, plan ways to encourage specific people.

- Decide to spur on the speaker by taking notes, giving words of encouragement throughout the message and being attentive. This is not a time to be passive, to sit back and wait to be stirred.

- Sing with all your heart (no natural talent necessary for this one) and smile, encouraging the song leaders and the people around you.

- Especially during the communion, consider the body (your relationships in the church) and plan to resolve any differences you may have.

We All Need Spurring On

I remember a time in the ministry in Australia when I needed "spurring on" in a major way. Mike and I were leading the church in Sydney and overseeing the other churches in Australia and the South Pacific. But that year Satan had attacked me continuously, and I wore down. A woman I had raised up as a leader in the ministry began to show signs of severe mental problems. An abused past had created a deep-seated bitterness that began to rear its ugly head. She was used by Satan to discourage and torment me. I had major surgery that year, and the night before I went to the hospital she came into my bedroom and unloaded many deluded and hateful attitudes toward me. She even placed in my heart seeds of doubt as to my respect and submissiveness in my relationship with my husband.

The other problem was simply isolation. I didn't have a healthy perspective on what was happening because I was too close to the situation and there was no one who could give me objective advice. My confidence in leading plummeted. So, toward the end of that year when we went to a conference in London, I was insecure and weird. I was thinking our leaders were going to have a talk with me about getting out of the ministry, telling me I really couldn't handle it.

But much to my surprise, as our leaders sat with us in an English pub, my sister in Christ rebuked me strongly with a passion I could not misunderstand. She "spurred" me on by speaking the truth to me. She told me I needed to change and put to death my insecurity and fearfulness. I knew she was right, and I began to repent. I put all my heart and soul toward becoming godly, diligent and confident in the ministry. Because of God's grace, Mike and I are still in the ministry, and now he serves as an elder in Washington, D.C. Also, the sister which Satan used to discourage me has repented, is faithful and is doing well.

Let us always be acutely aware of the great spiritual battle in which we are involved as we demolish every stronghold and take captive every thought to make it obedient to Christ (2 Corinthians 10:4-5). Let us continually love each other enough to "spur each other on toward love and good deeds."

LIFE APPLICATION

What would you say is your basic motivation for spurring others on to do good deeds? How can your motivation grow to be more and more like that of Jesus?

Honestly, how much time and energy do you spend in prayer for others, seeking direction and insight to help them grow? What specific decisions will help you take this area of your life to a deeper level?

How do you typically respond to being spurred on? Are you prideful? Defensive? Thankful? Joyful? Eager? Why should you have a positive response?

28 Confessing Sins to Each Other

DEAN FARMER
Hollis, New Hampshire

Therefore confess your sins to each other and pray for each other so that you may be healed....

James 5:16

"Stupid," "weak," "foolish" and a myriad of other words are used by people of the world to describe a person who is open and honest with sins or weaknesses. Most of us have been strongly and, sad to say, negatively influenced by experiences of openness before we became Christians.

"Oh no! What will people think of me?" "That's it! They won't like me any more since I told them the truth." "I can't be open about that; they will leave me!" These thoughts race through our heads like freight trains when we think about being open with what's really going on in our lives. Coupling these statements with past hurts and rejections, we feel hopeless and retreat further behind the masks we wear.

Some situations have so traumatized us that we find it almost unthinkable to be vulnerable again—all the while never growing or changing. We become discouraged because of our sins and weaknesses, or we become numb to them and rationalize why we can't change. We say, "It's not that bad" or "It's just a little sin" or "I don't need to be open." The result is that we come to accept our sin. But it is vulnerability that allows us to receive the much needed help and encouragement that God desperately wants to give his children. If we are to have a meaningful relationship with God and satisfying relationships with brothers and sisters in the body of Christ, we must throw out our worldly view of openness. We must trust God and take on his view.

God Works Only Through Openness

God has created us to function in a certain way. When we

sin, i.e. miss the goal, we mess up our relationships both with God and with people. All sin, whether we consider it "little" or "big," hinders us from functioning at full capacity as God has envisioned. It's like pouring a mixture of sugar and water into a Porsche and then wondering why it only goes 35 mph when it is designed to fly at 200 mph! When we continue in these sins, they eventually destroy our ability to have relationships with God and others. Just look at the divorce rate, crime rate and number of abused children, and you'll need no further proof.

All sin is extremely damaging to our bodies and minds (Galatians 5:19-21; Ephesians 5:3-5). The Bible describes what happens to us when sins are unconfessed and undealt with:

...my bones have no soundness because of my sin.
My guilt has overwhelmed me
    like a burden too heavy to bear.
My wounds fester and are loathsome
    because of my sinful folly.
My back is filled with searing pain;
    there is no health in my body.
I am feeble and utterly crushed;
    I groan in anguish of heart.
All my longings lie open before you, O Lord;
    my sighing is not hidden from you
My heart pounds, my strength fails me;
    even the light has gone from my eyes.
                    Psalm 38:3b-5, 7-10

Do you feel overwhelmed, burdened, tired or weak? Is there unconfessed sin? James 5:16 and the preceding verses show that sickness and sin can go hand in hand. (Although it is clear that not all sickness is due to sin. Legitimate sickness is legitimate sickness.) I have seen people complain about being overly tired when their situation in life would not necessarily have warranted it. Almost always, the sin would later come out: cheating on exams, sexual immorality, lying, etc. And almost always "the light was gone from the eyes" of these Christians.

One of our biggest problems is that we confess the "big" sins but we ignore the "smaller" ones. This is extremely dangerous to our spirituality. If we ignore the "little" cold our 6-month-old has, it could become pneumonia and he might die! Don't ignore the warning signs of unconfessed sin!

The following is my top-ten list of sins that we normally consider unimportant and often do not confess: faithlessness, criticalness, giving a false impression (deceit), laziness, lack of discipline, irresponsibility (especially in paying bills), insecurity, impurity, unkindness and selfishness. Make a decision today to look at your life, find where these sins are hiding, then confess and deal with them!

From Personal Experience

A situation in my wife's life has helped me to see the blessings of openness. When we were asked to move to Germany to lead the Berlin church, my wife had been a Christian for more than four years. She had helped dozens of women, who were met by others, to become Christians and had accepted this as her role. Yet, she had been faithless in thinking that she could not personally meet someone who would become a Christian. She had great fear in being open about this. She thought she would be told that she could not lead the women of Berlin. She feared being thought of as weak.

When she decided to be open, what she received was the encouragement and direction she needed to help her overcome her sin. She found that there is an atmosphere of acceptance in the kingdom of God! Since that time Kim has seen many blessings from God due to her openness. One such blessing was meeting Mary, an actress who became a Christian.

Of course, Satan continued to tell her many lies : *You're an American. You don't speak their language. You're Jewish and living in Berlin!* She continued to be open with her sisters, asking them to go with her to share her faith. While nine-months pregnant, she introduced herself to a man who accepted her invitation to come to church. In approximately five weeks he became a Christian. Later, she helped my mom and dad become Christians! She is studying the Bible with two women whom she personally met, and during the past three months, she has had many visitors with her at church. Her life is living proof that God truly blesses openness and confession.

LIFE APPLICATION

Are you experiencing God's blessings of openness right now in your life? Be honest with God and yourself. If not, then what have you not considered important enough to confess? Make a decision today to be open and begin experiencing God's incredible blessings.

How often do you ask God to show you your sin so you can confess it to him and to others?

Are you afraid to see your sin? Do you fear it will hurt your self-esteem and diminish your self-worth? How can God's grace give you confidence and take away these fears?

When you have confessed sin to another disciple, how did it affect your relationship? How did it help you to know God's acceptance?

29 Forgiving Each Other

ADRIENNE SCANLON

Be kind and compassionate to one another, forgiving each other, just as in Christ God forgave you.

Ephesians 4:32

Our Father, God, in his holiness and perfection desires to forgive each and every one of us. He not only forgives the "little" things, he forgives the most wicked, evil thoughts and actions in the life of each penitent sinner. His divine nature *wants* to forgive us.

Sadly, as we examine our own lives and face the world in which we live, we are forced to admit that in our sinful, human nature we hold grudges, blame others, and grow more and more bitter as we grow older. Divorce divides us. Prejudice separates us. Hurt cripples us. Mistakes ruin us. But God gives us the opportunity to change all this. Forgiveness is one of the ways human beings have of imitating the divine.

The Divine Example

As he hung, dying, Jesus said, "Father, forgive them, for they do not know what they are doing" (Luke 23:34). Physically battered and abused, publicly mocked and humiliated, personally abandoned by those closest to him, Jesus suffered horribly. And yet, in his suffering, he did not give in to the sinful, human desire to accuse, blame or lash out in anger. In spite of the violent circumstances, his ravaged body and his emotions, his godly nature shone through, and he won the offer of forgiveness for his accusers and for all mankind.

The Divine Expectation

Jesus left us an example that we should follow. In Matthew 6:14-15, Jesus warns us that if we do not forgive others, God will not forgive us. In Matthew 18:21-35, Jesus warns us that we will be severely punished if we do not forgive our brothers from our heart. We are told in Matthew 18:22 and Luke 17:4 that there is to be no limit to our desire to forgive one another. As we read the parable of the unmerciful servant (Matthew 18:21-35), Jesus shows us that those who will not forgive are ungrateful, hard-hearted, prideful and have forgotten that they, too, need to be forgiven. This attitude angers our Master! God expects repentance—a mind change! As disciples, we can decide to forgive other people. We don't have to be controlled by the negative circumstances, hurts and stormy emotions that entangle us.

The Daily Efforts

I live in a very densely populated city. Paris is home to more than ten million people! It is no surprise that I run into a few irritating, thoughtless, angry and hurtful people almost every day. It can also happen, in any given day, that a sister or brother will arrive late to an appointment, will forget to call me back or will speak to me unkindly. And, believe it or not, in my own home, I might find a husband who leaves his dirty socks on the floor or a child who responds to me angrily or disrespectfully.

Our daily lives are punctuated with irritations and inconveniences that come in all shapes and sizes. While we need to help all those around us (the lost and the saved) deal with their sin, we must also guard our hearts and our minds from anger, frustration, criticalness, self-righteousness and impatience. Learning to forgive each other on a daily basis is essential in the building of a Christlike character.

Three daily keys:
- *Prayer:* I pray daily (Luke 11:4) to have a forgiving attitude as I go through the day. I also talk to God about everyone that I need to forgive.
- *Perspective:* I remember that I have been, and still need to be, forgiven (Colossians 3:13). I have no right before God to hold a grudge.
- *Politeness:* I set my mind to respond with kindness and compassion (Ephesians 4:32) whenever I feel mistreated.

The Daring Efforts

The Christlike character that God builds in us, as we respond in a godly way to our daily challenges, gets tested as we face life's larger storms. Could we forgive a doctor who made a mistake during an operation and permanently handicapped our child? Could we forgive our husband or wife if they were unfaithful to us? Have we forgiven the parent (or teacher, or uncle) who mistreated or abused us as a child? Have we forgiven the friend who has betrayed or forgotten us? My prayer is that every disciple can answer these questions with a sober, whole-hearted, "Yes."

Recently a sister in Paris was confronted with the news of her parents' divorce. The family that she had always believed to be loving and united began to crumble. Her father, whom she had always believed was faithful to her mother, was dying of AIDS. After facing all this sadness, she also learned that her father had knowingly infected her mother with the killer disease. Anger. Disappointment. Rage. Sadness. Fear. Shame. How could she handle such pain? She began with kindness and compassion. When no one else in the family was willing to talk to her father, she and her husband took him into their home and their lives. She loved and forgave him in spite of the violent persecution from the rest of the family. He began to study the Bible and today he is a disciple and knows not only his daughter's love and forgiveness, but God's love and forgiveness as well.

Often, as Christians, we must dare to forgive as the world does not and cannot. The forgiveness that Jesus teaches us on the cross is "foolishness to those who are perishing" but brings us the power to love even those who have hurt and betrayed us (1 Corinthians 1:18). I am reminded of Stephen, the first of our many brothers and sisters who were martyred for their faith (Acts 7:54-59). He demonstrated the character of one who had made daily efforts to forgive as Christ did. He dared to die as Jesus died—with a pure and forgiving heart. As he died, he said, "Lord, do not hold this sin against them" (Acts 7:60). Let us, like Stephen, look to heaven, humble ourselves and strive to forgive one another deeply from the heart.

Do you pray daily to have a forgiving attitude as you go through the day? Do you talk to God about everyone you need to forgive, or do you stuff your feelings, not admitting you need to forgive someone?

How can prayer help you be more focused on your need to forgive others?

Do you remind yourself often that you have been, and still need to be, forgiven (Colossians 3:13)? How will this reminder help you to show forgiveness to others? To give up grudges that you hold?

How well do you set your mind to respond with kindness and compassion (Ephesians 4:32) whenever you feel mistreated? What is the effect on you and on the other person when you do this?

30 Offering Hospitality to One Another

Offer hospitality to one another without grumbling.
1 Peter 4:9

Paul says it simply and clearly in Romans 12:13, "Practice hospitality." The church-supported widow is to practice it (1 Timothy 5:10). The aspiring elder is to practice it (1 Timothy 3:2; Titus 1:8). All disciples are to practice it—young or old, single or married, male or female.

Certainly, some people are more talented in the area of serving, which includes hospitality. But as with most gifts from God, it is only their exercise that brings about growth and maturity. It is my firm conviction that all disciples can and must grow in the gift of serving and being hospitable as we reach out and influence the fragmented world in which we live. For elders, and those who have their hearts set on being an elder, God says we *must* be hospitable.

A good working definition of hospitality is having the heart and making the effort to meet the needs of others, both family and strangers. All people have the same needs—to feel warmly loved, enjoyed, appreciated and included. Our homes, apartments, flats, town houses, condos and all our belongings are gifts to us from our generous heavenly Father, who intends for us to use them to further his purpose. All the material blessings we receive from God can be either a tremendous strength in our expression of hospitality or a tremendous weakness as we consume ourselves in fulfilling our own pleasures and comforts.

Hospitality goes beyond the courtesy of rising and greeting people as they enter our home (though important). It goes beyond preparing and sharing a meal with others (though important). Hospitality is about going to great lengths to make our guests feel special. It means organizing the details, creating an atmosphere and making conversation with them in mind. By having our focus on our guests and their interests, they clearly feel special and loved.

Married Disciples

To be hospitable as a married couple requires a team effort. Linda and I make it a practice to both answer the door and greet our guests upon their arrival. Before this, while Linda is preparing the meal (I know my limitations), I take care of last-minute details that are important to both of us—running the vacuum one last time, straightening the pillows on the sofa, selecting appropriate music, or checking the room temperature. If children are included in the evening, which we encourage in order to build a feeling of family, we arrange our child-sized table and chairs for their use. As my talented wife puts the finishing touches on a well-planned and delicious meal, I take drink orders, fill glasses with ice, pour coffee and generally act the host. If additional items are needed after being seated, I will as likely get them as Linda. When our guests arrive, and as they share a meal with us, we want them to experience a time that has obviously been planned and arranged with their needs and comfort in mind.

A Few Thoughts for Singles

Singles need to work on making their houses or apartments a home, and their relationships a family. This begins with everyone deciding that the current arrangement is to be enjoyed instead of seeing it as a temporary, less-than-ideal holding pattern. Living quarters should be kept clean and ordered so that they are inviting and hospitable to others. Decisions need to be made and standards need to be set for daily upkeep. Many singles are on a limited budget as they are finishing school or just getting started in a career; therefore, they do not have much money to put into furnishings or decorations. This calls for some creativity so that the place in which they live does not have a drab atmosphere, but an encouraging one.

If singles, both men and women, see their living situations as simply a place to grab a quick sleep and a quick eat, then disorder, dust, depression and disunity and are bound to reign. This is hardly an atmosphere in which to experience family or to "practice hospitality" (Romans 12:13). No matter where we live or how long we live there, we are to share with other people. This is a mark of disciples of Jesus in all life situations.

The Heart of Hospitality

There are several forces working against us in achieving the level of hospitality that God expects. Most of us today have not been trained by our parents or by society to take responsibility for being hospitable. Etiquette is thought to be a relic of some past civilization. Actually, etiquette is a set of guidelines that define courtesy. Surely we can go overboard with rules of proper social behaviors, but being a gracious host and showing courtesy and respect through our hospitality is simply a display of love—a love that is "not rude" (1 Corinthians 13:5).

As disciples, we must constantly strive to overcome the sin of self-centeredness. This sin causes a variety of problems for us and can certainly limit or prevent our growth in being hospitable. A heart that is set on protecting our leisure time, recreation time, private time or family-alone time is not a heart that is striving to excel in the grace of hospitality. Certainly, it is important that we plan time to be alone with God, our spouse and our family, but the heart of a hospitable disciple is always planning times to meet the needs of others as well.

Many strong disciples, both married and single, will quickly say that the generous hospitality of people in the church has made a difference in their decision to come to faith and remain faithful during difficult times. Hospitality is part of the encouraging and shepherding aspect of God's heart and of the heart of his family. When we are too busy to be hospitable and to share our homes with others, disciples and nondisciples, we are simply too busy. Let us imitate the hospitable heart of our risen Lord as he lovingly prepared breakfast for his disciples and as he later returned to his Father's house to prepare rooms for us all.

Editors' note: This chapter has been adapted from Chapter 10 (Ron Brumley's chapter) in The Fine Art of Hospitality, *Sheila Jones, editor (Woburn, Massachusetts: Discipleship Publications International, 1995).*

LIFE APPLICATION

Would you say that offering hospitality is a strength of yours? In what ways can you grow in obeying this command?

In growing up, what was your experience with hospitality? Was the home in which you were raised open to people? In what ways do you want to imitate your experiences as a child and in what ways do you not want to imitate them?

God very much wants his disciples to be concerned about meeting the needs of others. When asked to think of a great example of someone who does this, who comes to mind? How can you imitate this person?

31 Honoring One Another

RICHARD BELLMOR

> Love must be sincere. Hate what is evil; cling to what is good. Be devoted to one another in brotherly love. Honor one another above yourselves.
>
> Romans 12:9-10

Imagine this: It's the evening of the Academy Awards. Millions of viewers are tuned in. Hundreds of photographers are present. Who will get the awards for Best Director, Actor and Actress? What will they be wearing? What will they say in their acceptance speeches? Wouldn't you be taken aback if a winner stepped up to the podium and said, "It's about time the Academy has recognized my true greatness after all these years. I alone have made myself into the success that stands before you today." It's safe to assume we would be shocked by their arrogance.

Equally shocking, even appalling, is a disciple who behaves this way. "I alone am responsible for the changes that have taken place in my life. I am able to handle my life without the help of anyone else."

Listen now to the heart of a disciple who really knows what it means to "honor one another." "Sister, you are an incredible leader." "Brother, that was a convicting message; I want to imitate your faith and conviction." "I really respect that couple for their decision to sacrifice so much for the kingdom." "Brother, because of your impact on me, I've changed so much." Are these the kind of statements you make to and about others in the body of Christ? Is your heart filled with gratitude and respect for the men and women around you? Webster's dictionary defines "honor" as follows: "to hold a person in high regard" or "to treat with great respect." How can honor become a characteristic of your relationship with others in Christ?

God First

My salvation and my honor depend on God;
he is my mighty rock, my refuge (Psalm 62:7).

Honoring one another begins by honoring God first. Most of us have spent a lifetime honoring ourselves. We have wanted others to think of us as the smartest, the most talented or the best-looking. When we first placed our eyes on Jesus, however, this desire to honor ourselves began to fade. We began to desire to honor someone far greater than ourselves. This desire to honor God must grow stronger every day. We must long to see God honored, glorified and lifted up for all that he does and has done! We must no longer worry about what people think of us, but rather what people think of God! We must be like Phinehas who was zealous for the honor of his God (Numbers 25:11-13). And we must not follow the example of Eli who was rebuked because he honored his sinful sons more than he honored God (1 Samuel 2:29).

It is amazing how much my own life and relationships have changed as my respect and honor for God has grown. I really do want to see God glorified more than myself and to see his plans succeed more than my own. It is truly a freeing moment when you can hold God in higher honor than you hold yourself.

Others Next

Honor one another above yourselves (Romans 12:10).

My three-year-old daughter, Cassidy, illustrates what it means to honor her dad. The conversation goes like this:
"Daddy, I love you."
"I love you too, honey."
"I love you three, Daddy."
"I love you more, honey."
"I love you the most, Daddy."
What just happened? A desire to honor one another above ourselves! We can mouth encouraging words sometimes, but is that truly what we feel in our hearts?

In a workshop last year, my wife, Bernadine, and I discussed what our goals in our closest relationships must be. We decided that it was our goal to make those who lead us successful, and by doing so we, ourselves would be successful. We inspired each disciple to make their leaders successful, and assured them that in so doing, they would also be successful. Too often we are only concerned with ourselves. Real success comes from making others successful. Jesus humbled himself before others. He took the heart of a servant and an attitude of bringing honor to God. As a result, Jesus shared in God's glory and honor (Philippians 2:5-11).

We have led the church in Rhode Island for the last four years. What amazes us most and makes our work such a joy is the way the disciples in the church love each other. We are truly a family. The Greek word Paul uses for brotherly love is *storge*, meaning "family love." We love and honor one another because we are family. We believe the best about each other. We ask each other for advice about our ministries, our families and our lives. These are not superficial relationships; we speak the truth to each other and have hard talks when needed. But underneath it all, we honor each other, and we really like each other. We affirm and build up each other. It is a joy to know that as we honor each other in our relationships, we bring honor to our God.

Practical Suggestions

- Make a decision to love the ministry of Jesus more than your position. This destroys sinful competition.
- Never allow a disagreement or misunderstanding to persist. Get together and talk things out. Your respect for the other person will increase instead of decrease.
- Become comfortable in building others up. Be known as an encourager.
- Take time to appreciate what others have done for you. This will create gratitude and destroy criticalness.
- Imitate those who have the character of showing honor to God and one another.

LIFE APPLICATION

How do you react when someone else is asked to do something that you think you can do better? Do you decide to encourage them?

Is it easy for you to give someone else credit? How often do you build up others for things they are doing?

Would you say your leaders feel honored by you? What do you think would cause them to feel honored?

Do you easily affirm others for helping you to grow spiritually? Why or why not?

Glory in the Church

> Now to him who is able to do immeasurably more than all we ask or imagine, according to his power that is at work within us, to him be glory in the church and in Christ Jesus throughout all generations, for ever and ever! Amen.
>
> Ephesians 3:20-21

"God in flesh." "Power in weakness." "Treasure in jars of clay." "Glory in the church." Do you see the parallels? In this book, we have looked at what the church can be and needs to be. But from one perspective the church is human, fragile and weak. Most of us have experienced this side of her nature in personal and memorable ways. We would be naive and unrealistic (and eventually disillusioned) if we tried to ignore this reality. But there is another truth that must be seen with eyes of faith: The church is also divine. She is called out *by God* and uniquely touched *by God*. As Paul puts it in Ephesians 3, God's power is "at work within us." We know from other biblical passages that this power is nothing less than God's own Spirit (Romans 8:9; 1 Corinthians 3:16) which he has poured into our lives. Glory belongs to God, but God has picked us out and betrothed himself to us. He has wedded himself to us. He has given himself to us. And because of that gracious decision on his part, his glory can be seen in this world through those of us who are now his church.

In Jars of Clay

Philip Yancey in his book *Disappointment with God* tells of a friend who has cerebral palsy. Her mind is bright and quick, but her body will not always do what that sharp mind tells it to do. Sometimes the unpredictable actions of her body are an embarrassment and a humiliation to her. Yancey finds in her situation a metaphor for the church. God has chosen to risk humiliation and embarrassment by putting himself into us who are jars of clay, into us who are sometimes emotionally fragile, into us who can be prideful and self-deceived, into us who will always make some mistake if given enough time.

In the case of his friend, some may quickly dismiss her as one who has little to offer; but others, who spend enough time to get to know her, see her determined mind and heart shining through. Someone who looks at the church may see only average people with commonplace conflicts and typical weaknesses, and tend to dismiss her. I am writing this on a morning after being with the church on the previous night. I have to admit there was nothing outwardly impressive about most of us who were in that assembly. A snapshot of our group would have revealed some unusual diversity of race and age, but beyond that, we would be known for our ordinariness. But a closer and longer look reveals much more. Beneath the humanness, something divine shines through in any church that truly belongs to God. Grace, self-denial, compassion, honesty and unselfish concern are all preached and practiced. They are practiced imperfectly, but they are practiced with determination and sincerity. Love is replacing distrust. Forgiveness is overcoming bitterness. Sacrifice is replacing selfishness. Faith is pushing out cynicism. And more and more people are being added each week to this scene of transformation.

The fellowship of which I am part is no more perfect than I am; we are a work in progress. But I see God and his glory shining through. I routinely see some things I would see in the world only rarely. I often see other things I would never see in the world at all; they are produced only by the power of God. There is glory in the church!

Ever-Increasing Glory

As long as the world lasts, we will be able to see the humanness of the church. Just as Philip Yancey's friend must accept her condition, and must realize that certain aspects will not change, so we must accept our condition: In this world we will be human. But, having written those words, I quickly realize that at this point the metaphor breaks down. While the church must accept the fact that the glory of God will always be manifested through our humanness, we must never simply accept our weaknesses and failings. Our goals must be great ones. We must always be asking Christ to make us stronger, to change us, to help us become more of a true reflection of him. With faith that we can be different, we must be devoted to the discipline required for spiritual growth. Such hunger and thirst for righteousness will not go unfulfilled (Matthew 5:6). If we ask, seek and knock, it will be given to us, we will find, and the door will be opened (Matthew 7:7-8). When we pursue God, we will be transformed with "ever-increasing glory" into his likeness (2 Corinthians 3:18).

I have found it amazing how the most ragtag of groups can accomplish remarkable things when they have inspirational leadership. David took a group of 400 who were "in distress or in debt or discontented" and led them to victory after victory (1 Samuel 22:2ff). But as we have seen, the church is led not by a great human leader, but by the Son of God himself. As long as our eyes are fixed on him and as long as we are determined to let his word be supreme among us, extraordinary things will happen. His leadership will override our weakness. His divine nature will lift us above our human nature. He will do through us "immeasurably more than all we ask or imagine."

So, love the church. Jesus does.

Be thankful for the church. It is the one body of Christ on earth.

Never give up on the church. He never will.

Work for the perfecting of the church. Jesus is doing that at this moment.

Give your very life for the church. Sacrifice to see her have a dynamic presence in every nation, every city, every town, every village. That is exactly what Jesus did.

Have the same attitude toward the church that you find in Christ Jesus. Bind yourself tightly to others who do the same. And you will see things that prophets and kings longed to see. You will see "glory in the church and in Christ Jesus throughout all generations! Amen"!

T.A.J.

Who Are We?

Illumination Publishers International (IPI Books) began publishing in 2003. It was begun by Toney C. Mulhollan and is affiliated with churches committed to following the Bible and making disciples of all nations. It publishes and distributes materials that honor God, lift up Jesus Christ and show how his message practically applies to all areas of life. We have a deep conviction that no one changes life like Jesus and that the implementation of his teaching will revolutionize any life, any marriage, any family, and any single.

Since our begining we have published over 224 books and with the acquisition of Discipleship Publications International (DPI) several years ago, we now have over 330 titles and thousands of audio lessons and teaching series. More than three million volumes have been printed, and our works have been translated into more than a dozen languages.

You can find us at www.ipibooks.com. Download our IPI App for easy ordering. We appreciate the thousands of comments we have received from readers.

www.ipibooks.com

THE KINGDOM
OF GOD

VOLUME ONE

THE FUTURE BREAKS IN

Tom A. Jones and Steve D. Brown

Book by Tom A. Jones

THE KINGDOM OF GOD

VOLUME TWO

THE SERMON AND THE LIFE

Tom A. Jones and Steve D. Brown

Book by Tom A. Jones

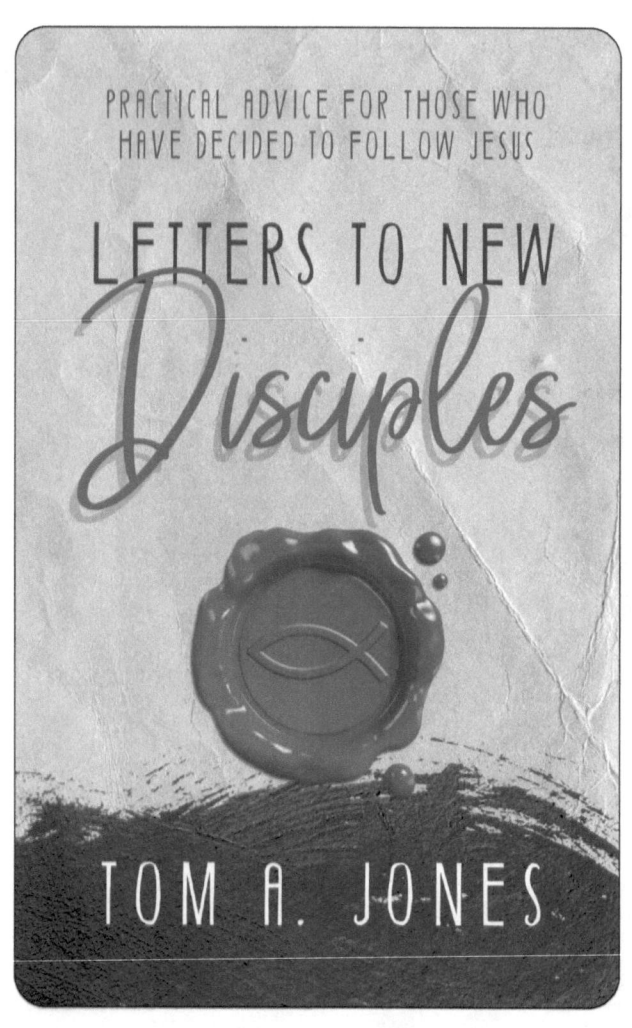

PRACTICAL ADVICE FOR THOSE WHO
HAVE DECIDED TO FOLLOW JESUS

LETTERS TO NEW
Disciples

TOM A. JONES

Book by Tom A. Jones